Charlotte Verity
Echoing Green: The Printed Year

with an introduction by Rachel Giles

Ridinghouse

Charlotte Verity

Echoing Green: The Printed Year

Contents

Some sort of luminosity

As my brush begins to find the right white for the Honesty,
I get a really strong sense of painting the moon.

Charlotte Verity[1]

During 2020 – a time of lockdown, birdsong and some of the clearest
blue skies ever seen in London – Charlotte Verity made a series of
watercolour monotypes inspired by what she saw in her garden.
She created them almost daily for the first three months; after that,
at least one a week. Through the seasons, foliage and flowers common
to British gardens appeared in succession: snowdrops, blossom, tulips,
roses, irises, nasturtiums, fuchsia, holly. Picking a stem of something
that caught her eye, Verity would take it up to her studio. She would
then paint it with watercolour directly onto Mylar plates, from which
monotypes were made.[2]

Printmaking is process, and nature is process. *Echoing Green* walks
us through the entire year: as we view Verity's prints we see the
seasons unfurl through the changing forms of flowers, branches
and leaves, and also through the gradual shifts in format and colour.
When she began in January, the prints were small in size, suiting the
diminutive snowdrops and violets they depict. By the time of the first
daffodils, the prints stretch upwards or outwards, with images in
daring triptych compositions. By summer, prints blossom into their
largest formats and the flowers are at their loudest. Then after the
golden hurrah of autumn, winter rolls in – and forms become simpler,
more spare.

January's prints are streaked with the slate grey of London skies
and the dark evergreen of holly. Spring is all hope and fervent activity:
the blue of those skies, blue-tit yellow, acid green, smudgy purple,
the lipstick pink of a tulip. By high summer, our retinas are dazzled
by the outrageous orange of Verity's nasturtiums and blood-red
fuchsias. Autumn's silver birch leaves are golden coins. Every print
has its own mood and atmosphere. Colour trumps form – in such an
unpredictable and loose medium as watercolour monotype, it is more
important to give a sense of the grape hyacinths' juicy, bluish purple
than to get the shape of its knobbled flowers absolutely precise.

Light permeates these prints. The white paper support has something to do with this, and gives the watercolour paint a surprising
luminosity. Light is also subject. In the springtime prints we have
glorious pale blue hues suggestive of the skies in Hans Memling
portraits, glimpsed through a window behind his sitter. Washes of

yellow suggest the watery glow of autumn sunlight; deep green and grey, the feeble light of winter dusk.

Although the flowers and plants of *Echoing Green* sit within a generously empty space, they are not wholly divorced from context, and they are paired with abstract hints of Verity's south-east London locale. The yellow stripe of a road marking. The form of a telegraph pole. The black of tarmac. These are signs of an urban milieu, not a rural idyll. Thus they have a sense of place about them, but not too much; enough for us to relate this project to our own experience. The tight crop around each subject also gives something of a sense of enclosure. Not claustrophobically so, but there is a containment, a place of laser focus within Verity's field of creativity and experimentation, a place she wants us to look.

There is a hopefulness about printing: you never know how it will turn out. There is a built-in delay between making the plate and seeing the result. Nature keeps us guessing, and there is a similar anxiety and expectation about printmaking.

ECHOES, GHOSTS

Printmaking is reflection, a reversal through time and space. In Verity's watercolour monotypes there is a further reversal. An image emerges not just from paint added, but from paint taken away: she removes freely washed-on areas of colour by drawing with a brush loaded with water, which brings unusual clarity and exactitude. Finding the edges of things, she gives shape to individual leaves, petals, reflections and thorns.

Most prints in the series combine at least two plates, and many combine more. When a plate is run through the press, most of the pigment is released from the plate into the dampened paper. What remains is called a ghost. In this series, she uses these plates to build up images, freely exploiting their residual colour, sometimes reversing them, or using them only partially. The ghosting lends each work a sense of depth, complexity and mutability, thus achieving a level of subtlety that is unique to this technique.

Images are often built up in layers using two or three freshly painted plates as well as the ghost of a previous image. *CV77* (p.103), for example, holds a clear memory of *CV66* (p.95). Some of the most complicated are the triptychs *CV26, 28* and *59* (pp.44–45, 48–49 and 84–85), which were made from nine plates in all. Two images of the same subject, one painted a day or two earlier, are sometimes combined in one print, such as in *CV4* (p.21). Others, for example *CV60* (p.86), are made up entirely of previously printed plates – echo upon echo. These techniques all give a strong sense of time's passage. Once a print had left the press, the artist's work was done. But having almost completed the series, Verity found that with prints she deemed too weak to survive on their own terms, she could paint on them with watercolour. *CV10W*, *CV19W* and *CV94W* (pp.29, 37 and 121) are examples of these hybrids. By using the traces of the original without obscuring them, she could make a completely new work.

In her studio, Verity placed in jars the flowers or foliage she had picked and set them on panes of glass, incorporating their reflections into the compositions. This reflection is another ghost, an alternative view, a way of bringing abstraction into the frame. It is untouchable, a spectral double of a physical object, something that shifts a flower from the realm of the observed still-life object into a more metaphysical space.

The prints echo in other ways. They are traces of a moment. In their composition, they are the reflections of a mood, an emotion or a glimpse of something – as Verity says, things that caught her eye and lifted her spirits. William Wordsworth describes these moments in Book XII of *The Prelude* as 'spots of time', experiences prompted by nature, which 'lifts us up when fallen':

> There are in our existence spots of time,
> That with distinct pre-eminence retain
> A renovating virtue, whence – depressed
> By false opinion and contentious thought,
> Or aught of heavier or more deadly weight,
> In trivial occupations, and the round
> Of ordinary intercourse – our minds
> Are nourished and invisibly repaired;
> A virtue, by which pleasure is enhanced,
> That penetrates, enables us to mount,
> When high, more high, and lifts us up when fallen.[3]

For Wordsworth, spots of time populated his earliest childhood, but Verity speaks of them as the small epiphanies she encounters in everyday life, the kind of revelations that Emily Dickinson describes so well. It is nature that seems to furnish us with many of these episodes, graciously gifting sparks of luminosity, no matter what is going on in the world around us or inside our minds.

The title of the series *Echoing Green* comes from William Blake's poem prompted by the sight and sound of children playing on a rural green in springtime. This is a poem full of auditory images – laughter, skylark and thrush-song, the peal of church bells. South-east London is a far from silent place, especially now lockdown is over. Listening to the recording of my interview with Verity when researching this essay, I heard the sounds of children from a school playground echoing around the nearby buildings and asphalt, which I had not noticed at the time. Later in the recording, I also detected the low rumble of a bin lorry. These moments were captured, along with our conversation about Verity's own recordings, impressions, and soundings. We add layer upon layer to our notations of experiences.

Poetry is crucial to Verity's work: 'It sets a standard for me … the place that painting can be aiming for.' She tests different kinds of paper by painting out the words of poems by Alice Oswald, Eavan Boland, John Clare and Wallace Stevens, among others. This is done with such care and artistry that it goes beyond something functional; to me it seems like a meditative act, a slow, conscious absorption of poetry into her painting. She arranges these poems on the table where she lays flowers or foliage, the crucible of her looking. They sit behind that spot of intense observation, arranged in a row as if forming a sort of altar.

While undeniably precise, Verity's work in this series is the antithesis of botanical painting. That can be precise too, and the result of long, hard looking. But the aim of botanical art is to show with scientific correctness a plant or a flower for the point of record. It occupies a zone apart from time and place. The hand of the artist is visible of course, but the purpose of the work is to explain. The difference with Verity's painting is her poetic imagination: the lucidity of her mind, as she sees and then represents something that has resonance for her. This is the impetus, the thing that makes her work occupy a different space from botanical art.

John Ruskin makes this distinction in the first volume of *Modern Painters*. In appropriately floral Victorian language, he writes that the artist must move beyond trying to depict botanical accuracy, and at this point a flower starts to speak: 'Thenceforward the flower is to [the artist] a living creature, with histories written on its leaves, and passions breathing in its motion.' The flower in an artist's work, he writes, is 'no mere point of colour, no meaningless spark of light. It is a voice rising from the earth, – a new chord of the mind's music,

– a necessary note in the harmony of his picture, contributing alike to its tenderness and its dignity, nor less to its loveliness than its truth.'[4]

Ruskin personifies the flower. It has a voice, it is expressive of 'the mind's music', a conduit of the artist's thoughts or feelings: a crucial part of showing emotional truth in a work of art. He writes of its dignity in unmistakably human terms. Verity says that she uses nature 'to make it resonate for fundamentals', which I take to mean that it creates reverberations, a language almost, to express the things that matter to her.

This is not to say that the flowers and plants in Verity's work are meant to be viewed as symbolic. Rather, they are echoes or impressions of her experience. Nor are they about the representation of beauty for the sake of it. Beauty in itself does not catch her attention: the irises in her garden, for example, have been left out of *Echoing Green*: 'One day I'll paint the irises, but it's more to do with finding, making something out of a glimpse of something. The glimpse is important to me.'

Representing flowers in art should not be dismissed as easy, as an 'amateur's subject', or as something particularly 'feminine'. Artists tell me repeatedly that depicting flowers is excruciatingly difficult; my book *Bloom: Art, Flowers and Emotion* shows that a good proportion of twentieth-century artists – many of whom were male – were preoccupied with this exact challenge.[5] Verity says that the risk an artist takes in depicting a rose is as nerve-wracking as trying to render a convincing portrait of a person: 'More than any other flower … you do it badly and disrespectfully … it turns into something so ugly … it can be terrifying.'

> Where is our comfort but in the free, uninvolved, finally mysterious beauty and grace of this world that we did not make, that has no price? Where is our sanity but there? Where is our pleasure but in working and resting kindly in the presence of this world?
>
> *Wendell Berry*[6]

While we were busy fretting about the R number and a constantly changing list of restrictions, nature carried on doing its thing, oblivious to our discomfort. For many of us in 2020, our lives became ostensibly smaller. But as is now clear, the lockdowns of 2020 also opened our eyes to what was always there: microcosms in our gardens, flowering weeds sprouting from pavement cracks, the verdant green of a local park, or flowers spilling out from a window box. Things were revealed to us during our regulatory hour of daily exercise that we had not seen before. But with her fierce gaze, Charlotte Verity already had a head start on the rest of us. Her prints capture this glimpsed world.

In 2020, our usual comings and goings, identities and modes of being were scratched out. What was then left but to watch 'this world that we did not make'? The progression of spring, summer, autumn and winter was a comfort; these are the echoes of years gone before, and will – climate change notwithstanding – be repeated in years to come. It is already becoming something of a cliché that 2020 was the year that brought us back into harmony with nature; yet as with all clichés, there is a hard kernel of truth.

Verity's body of work in *Echoing Green* brings us back into step with the cycle of life, and with the rhythms and seasons of a year. But the joy of her work is that she does not present us with some bucolic paradise that is out of reach for so many (in 2020, 83 per cent of Britain's population were living in cities).[7] Verity's environment is resolutely urban and presented in a visual language that we intuitively understand. Especially online, images proliferate: of ourselves, consumer products, celebrities, food, sunsets, the things we love. Verity shows us how to look again at the physical world and to invest in the value of slow looking, a lucid dreaming within a landscape that we did not entirely fashion ourselves. Ultimately she shows us, as Wendell Berry puts it, the natural world's 'mysterious beauty and grace'. Not an obsessively curated, Instagram-worthy surface beauty, but beauty with complexity and meaning.

In *Echoing Green*, each work takes one of Verity's 'spots of time' and transforms it with care and attention into something we can also experience. There are myriad things to see in her neighbourhood. In each one of these prints, there is some sort of luminosity, the light reflected by objects and the light of those unforgettably clear lockdown skies, the brilliance of Verity's poetry. There is space to draw breath: she is saying, 'Here, take a look at this. It is worth it.'

1 On painting *Lunaria*: *Charlotte Verity, A Year in Tradescant's Garden*, exhibition catalogue, Garden Museum, London, 2011, diary entry, 11 November 2010, p.26.

2 All quotations and paraphrases from Charlotte Verity are from my interview with her, which took place on 3 June 2021. The words 'some sort of luminosity' are Verity's.

3 William Wordsworth, *The Prelude XII* (1805), lines 208–18, at https://romantic-circles.org/editions/poets/texts/preludeXII.html, accessed 24 June 2021.

4 John Ruskin, *Modern Painters, Volume 1* (1843), John Wiley & Sons, New York, 1890, p.xxxvi.

5 Rachel Giles, *Bloom: Art, Flowers and Emotion*, Tate Publishing, London, 2020.

6 Wendell Berry, 'The Art of the Commonplace', in *The Agrarian Essays*, Counterpoint, Berkeley CA, 2002, p.215.

7 'United Kingdom – Urban Population (% Of Total)', at https://tradingeconomics.com/united-kingdom/urban-population-percent-of-total-wb-data.html, accessed 21 July 2021.

Plates

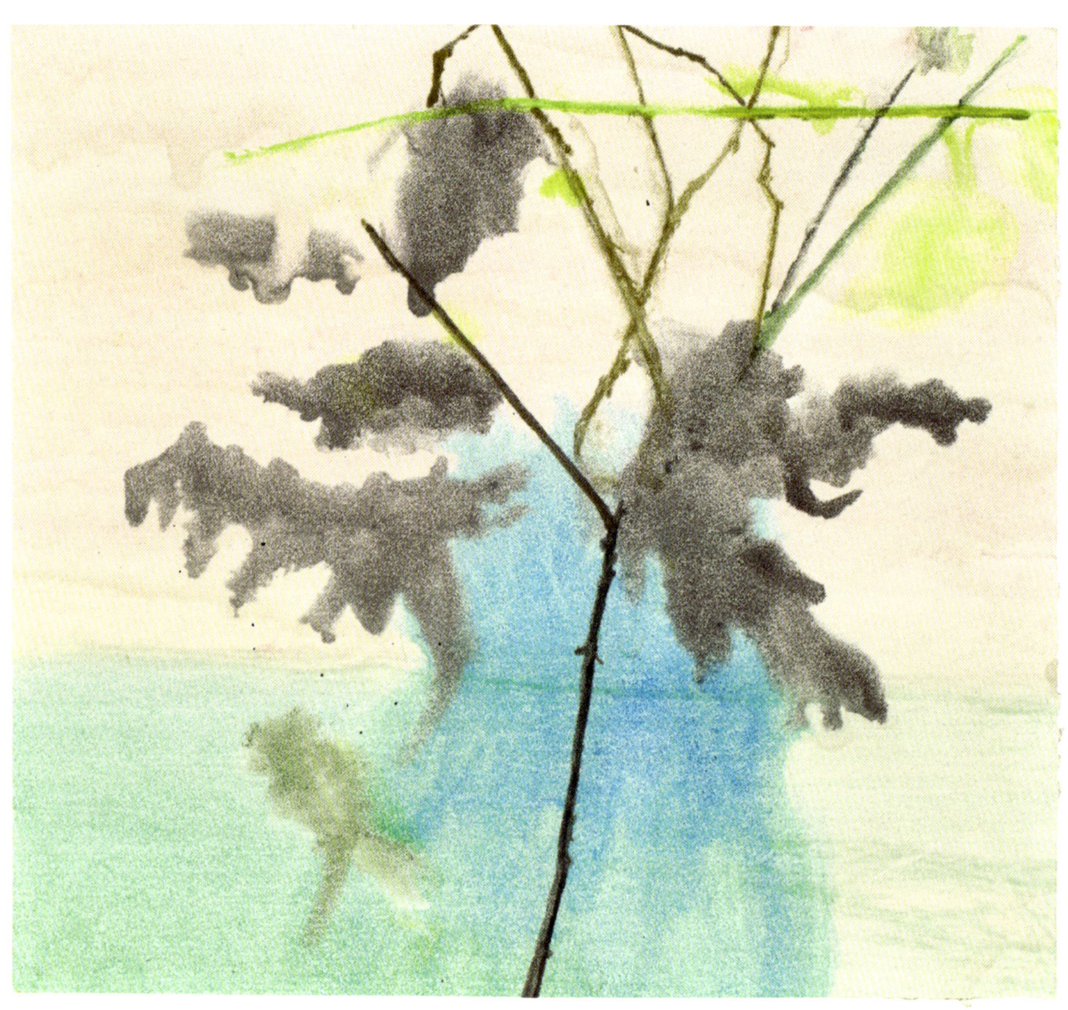

  CV1, 2020   watercolour monotype, 17.8 × 19.9 cm

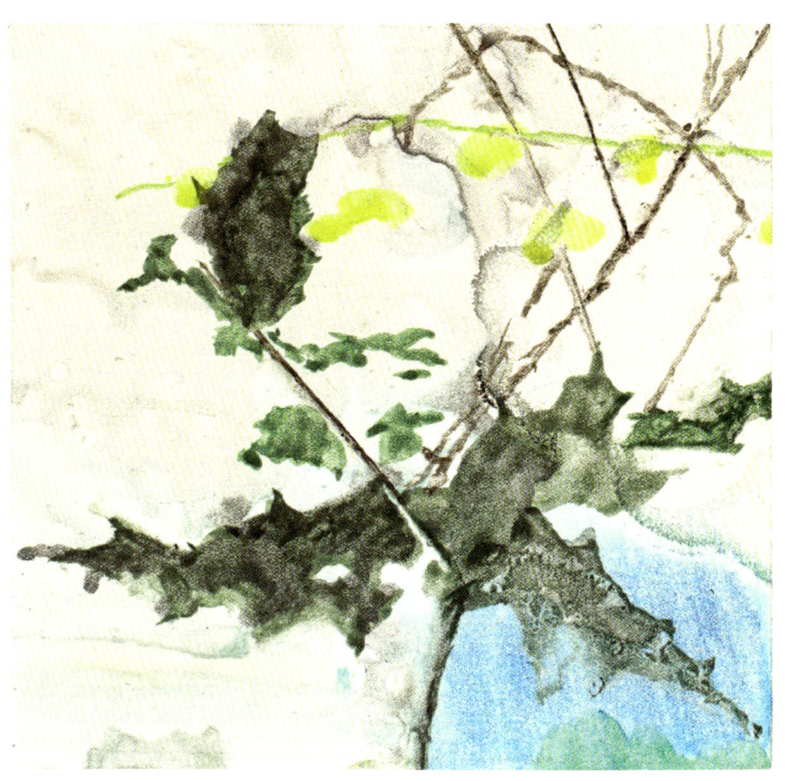

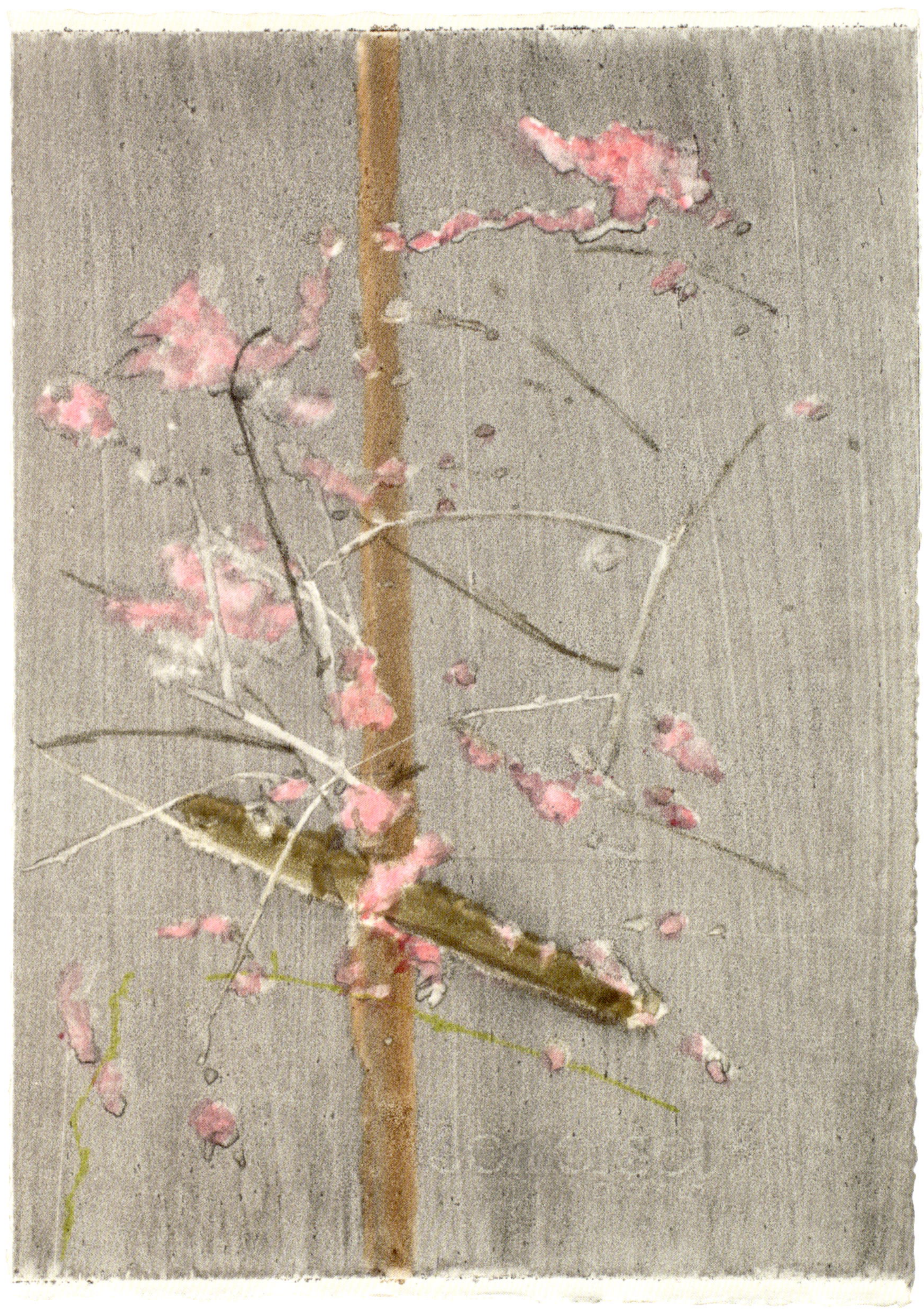

20   *CV3*, 2020   watercolour monotype, 28.8 × 20.7 cm

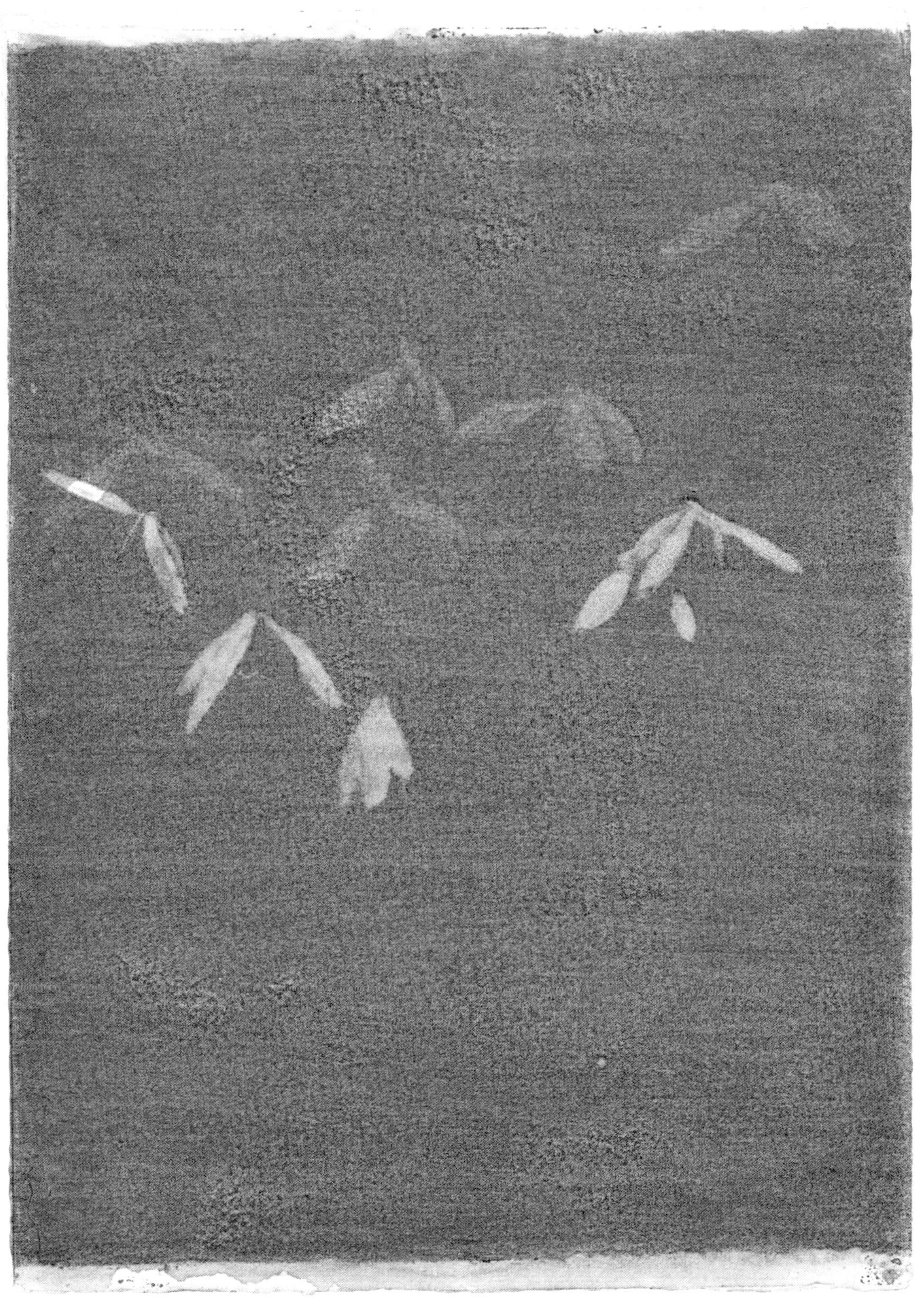

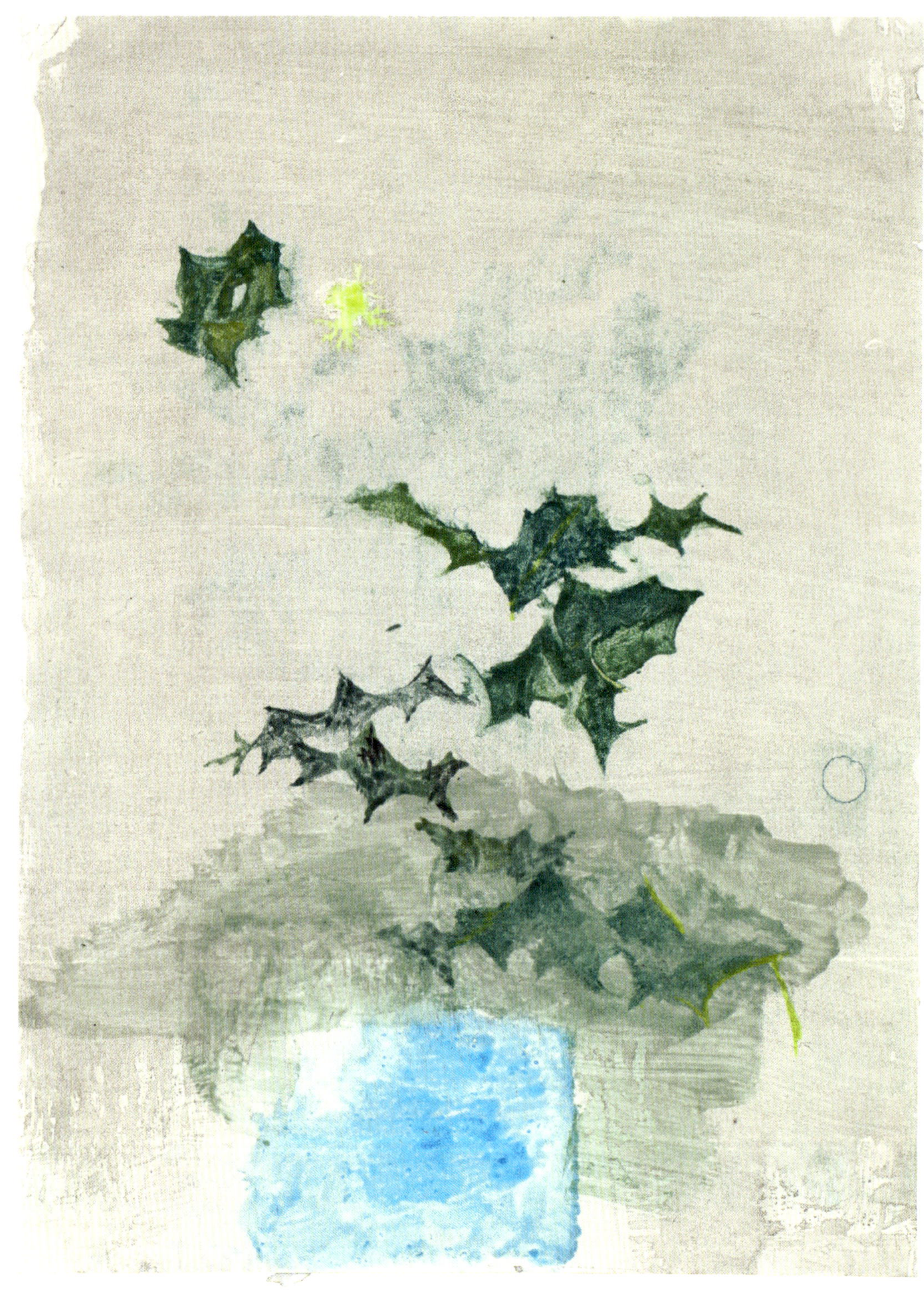

    CV5, 2020   watercolour monotype, 26.8 × 19.8 cm

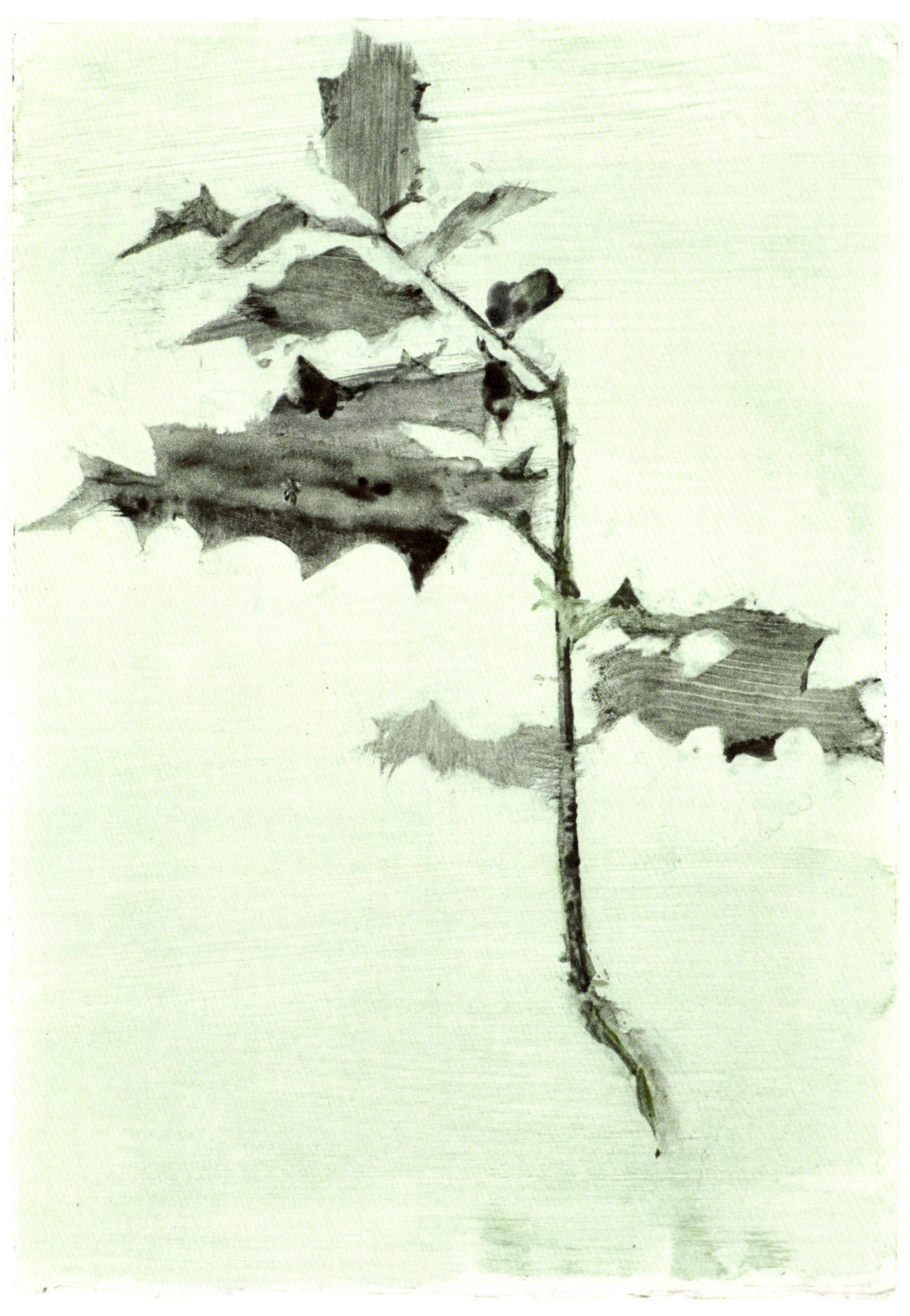

CV6, 2020   watercolour monotype, 28.8 × 20.8 cm   **23**

  CV7, 2020   watercolour monotype, 28.7 × 21 cm

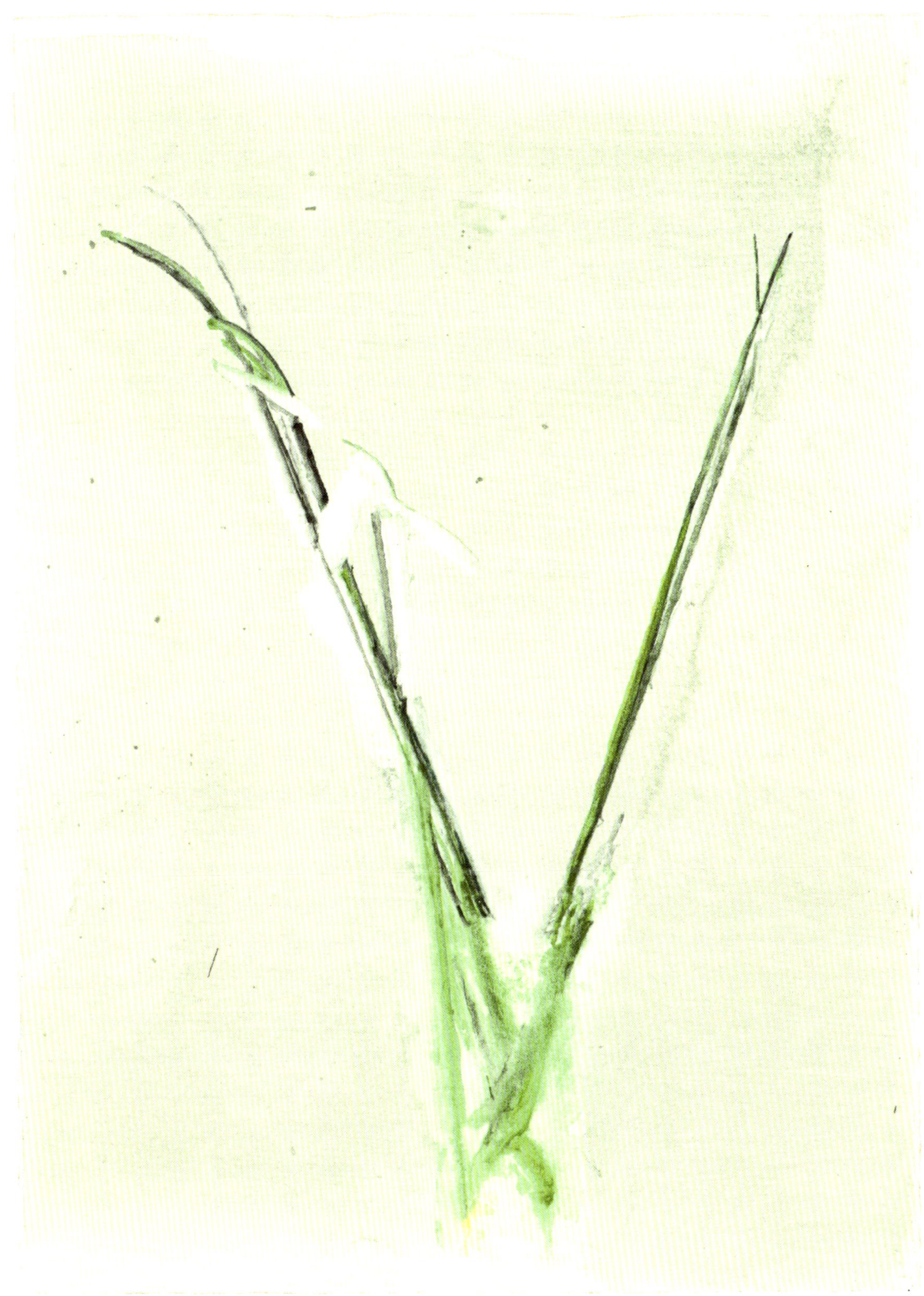

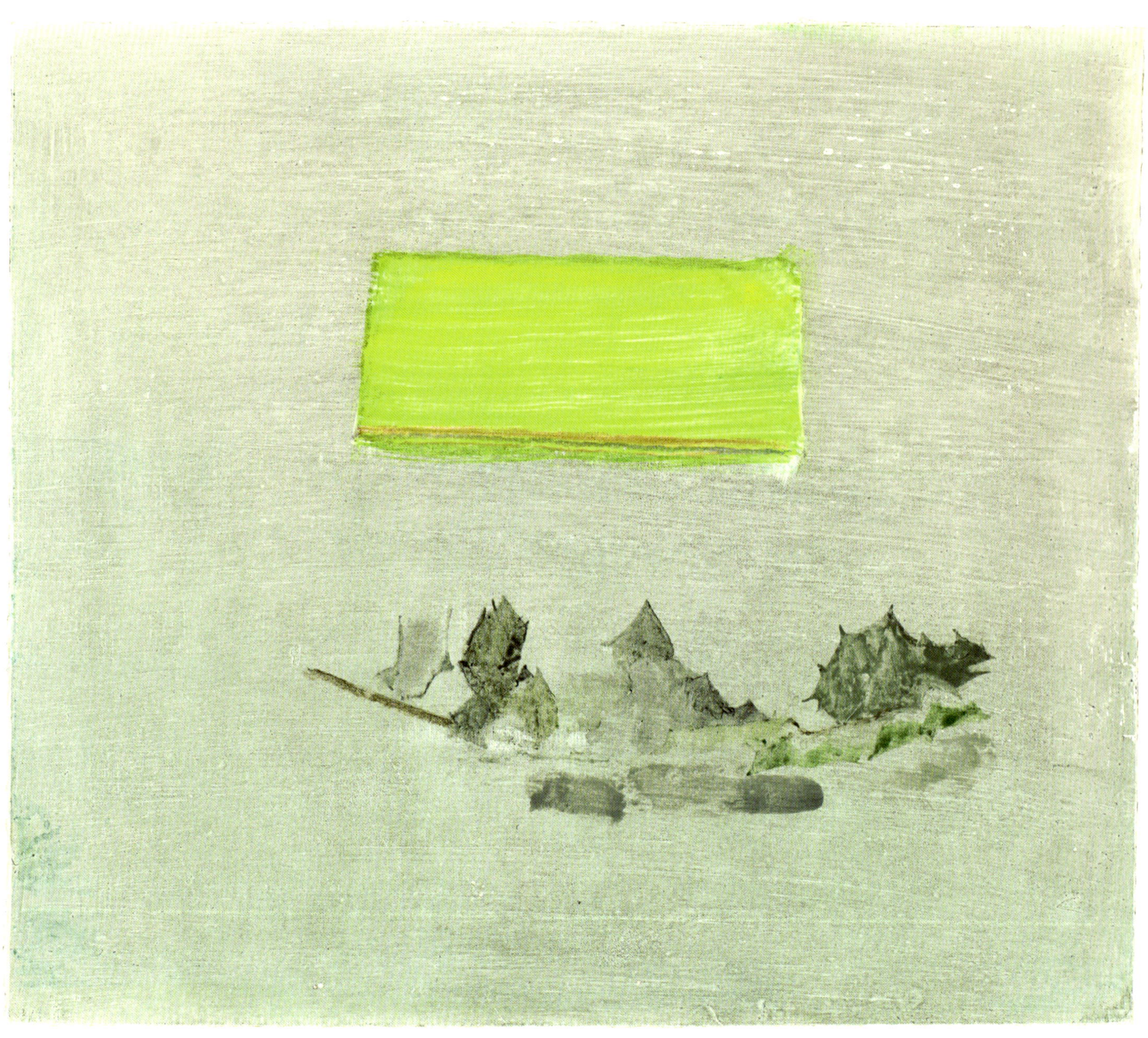

   CV8, 2020   watercolour monotype, 33.8 × 39.4 cm

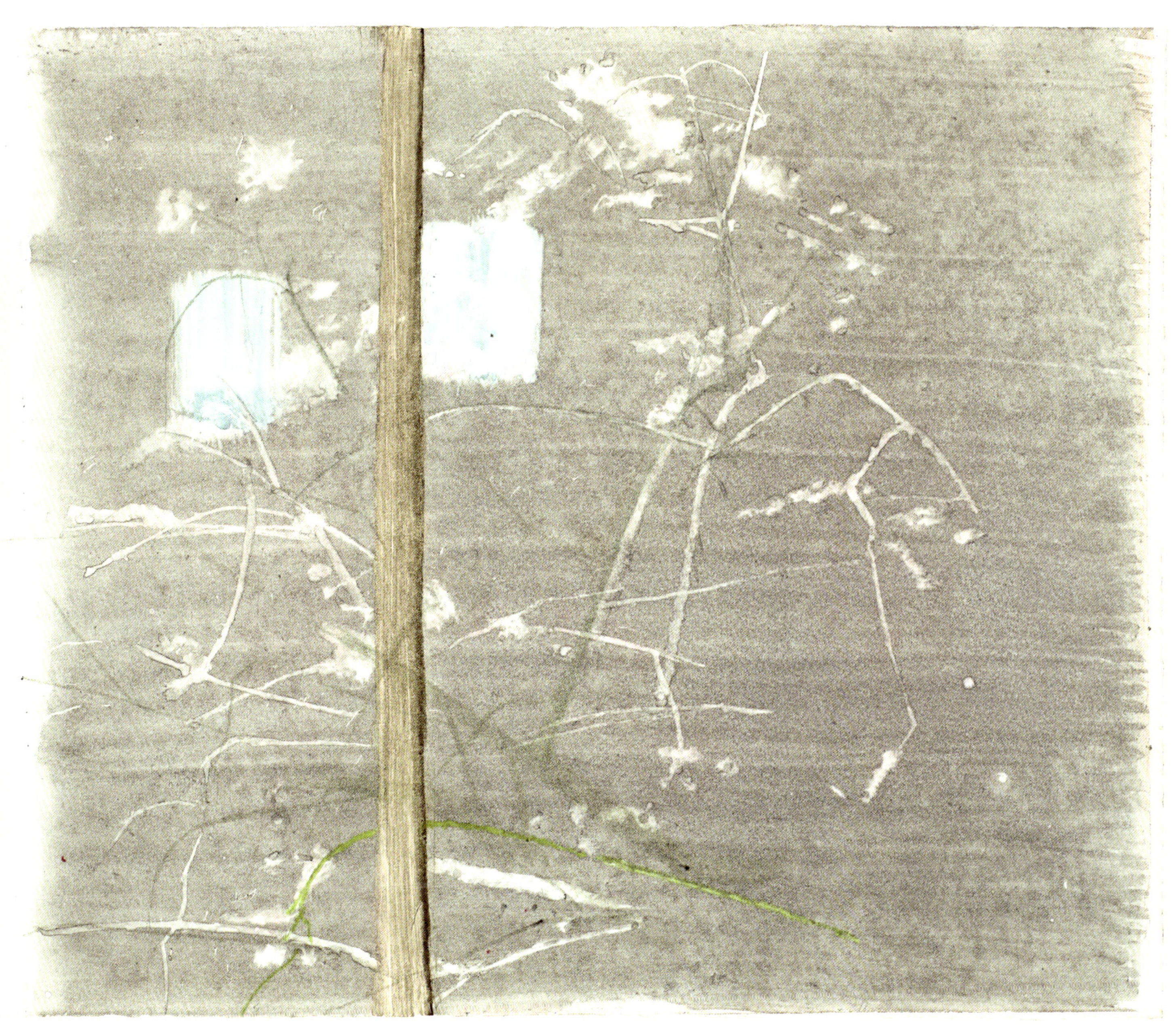

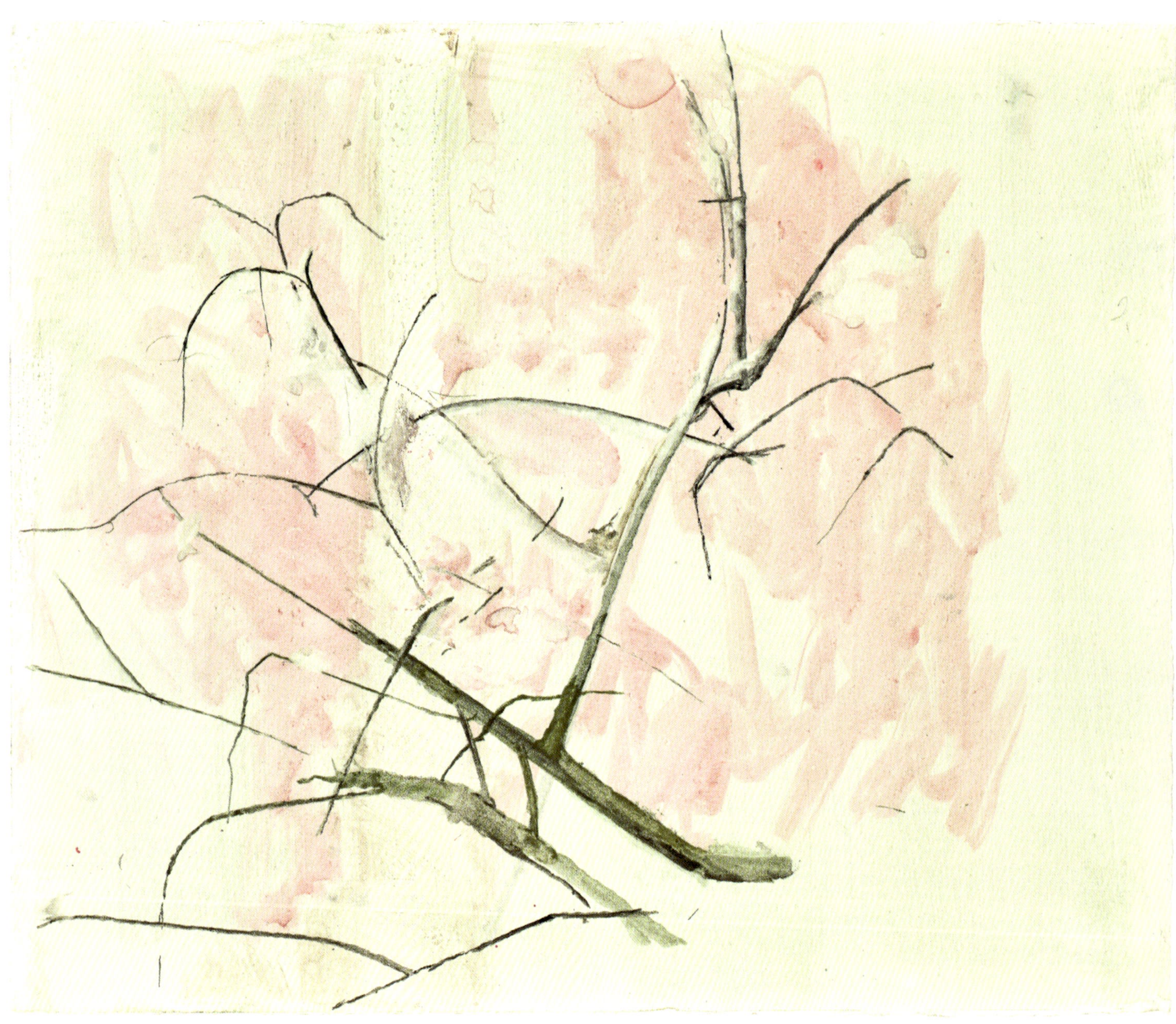

 CV11, 2020   watercolour monotype, 33.8 × 41 cm

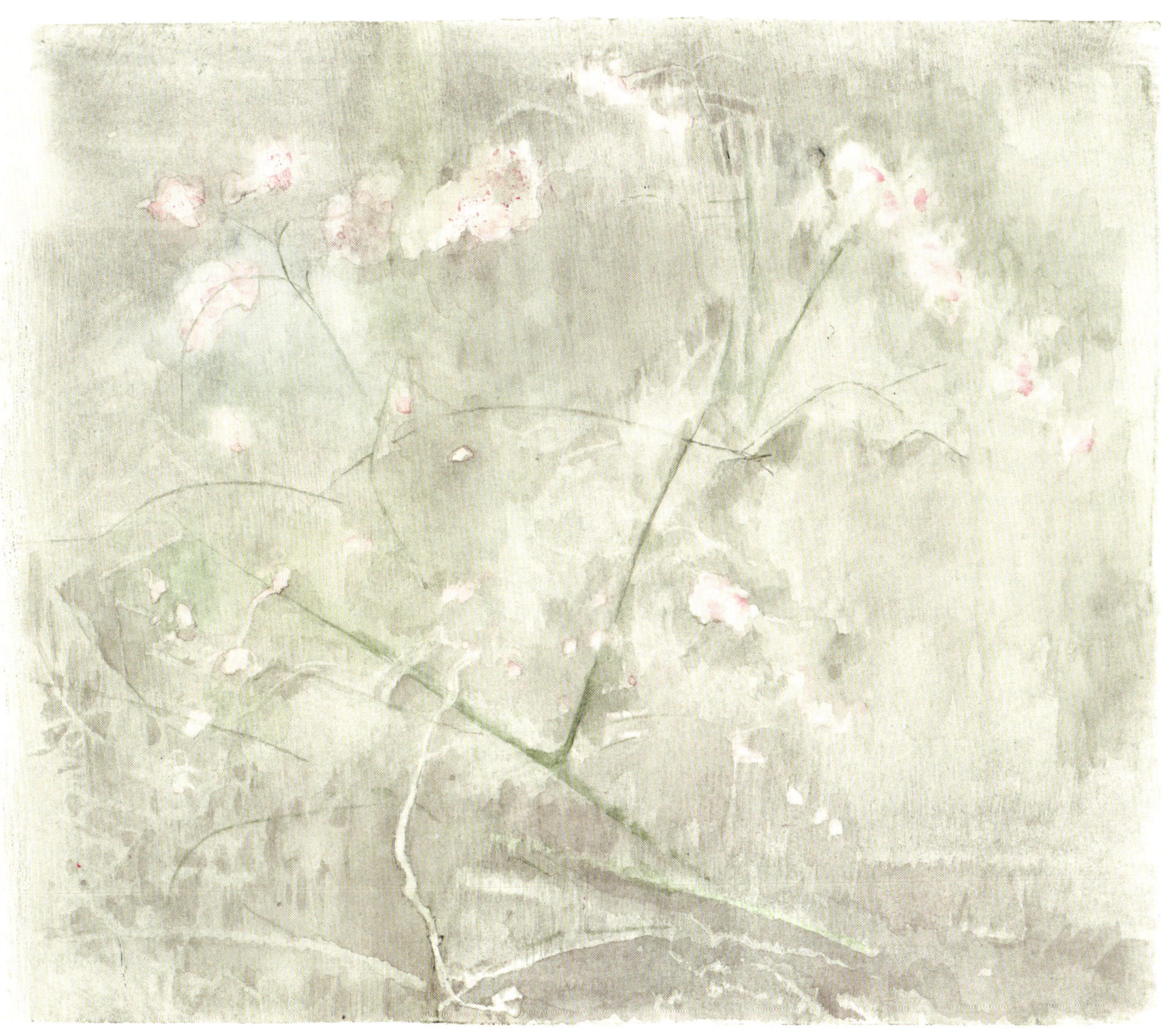

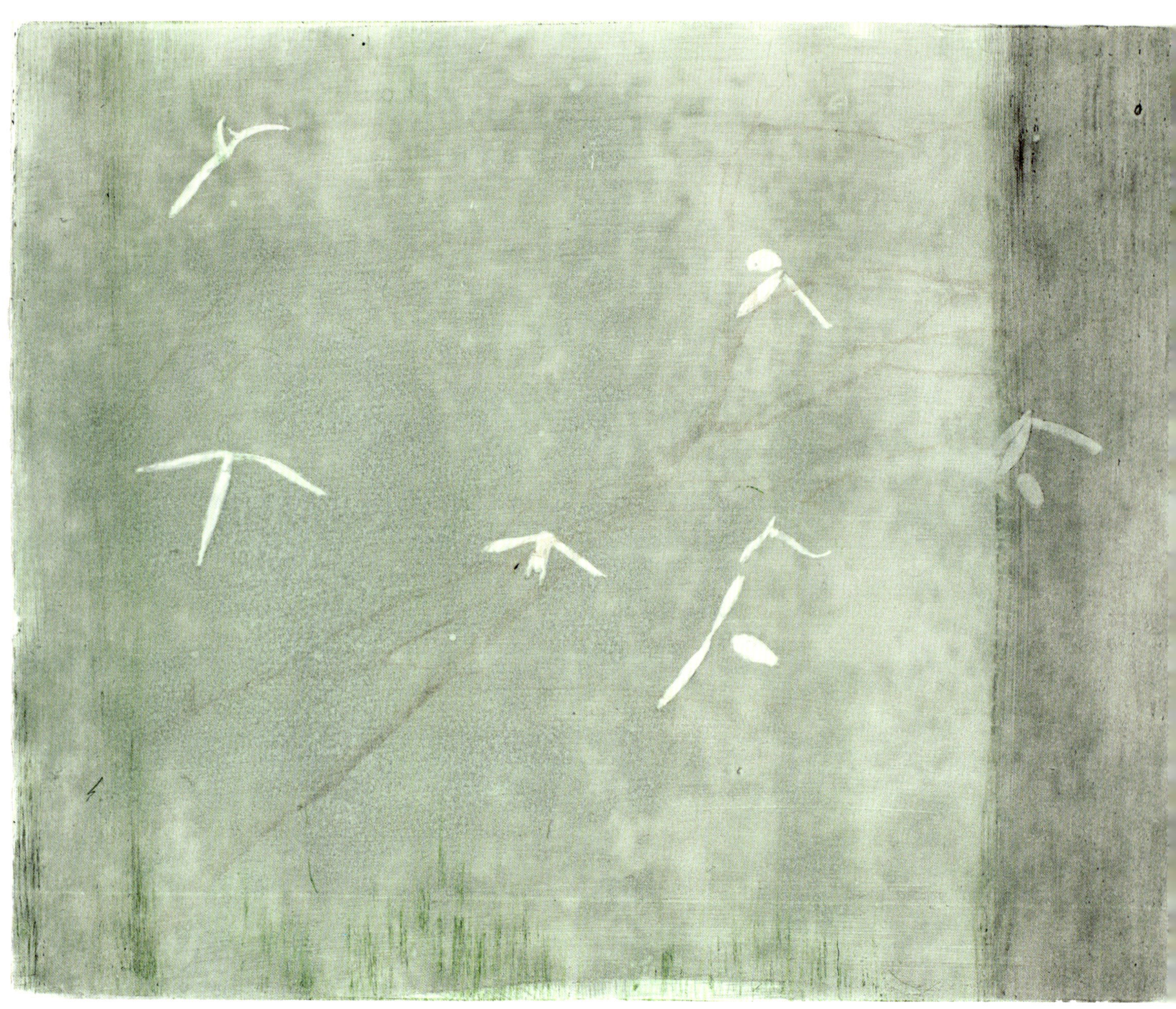

30   *CV13*, 2020   watercolour monotype, 32.7 × 40.5 cm

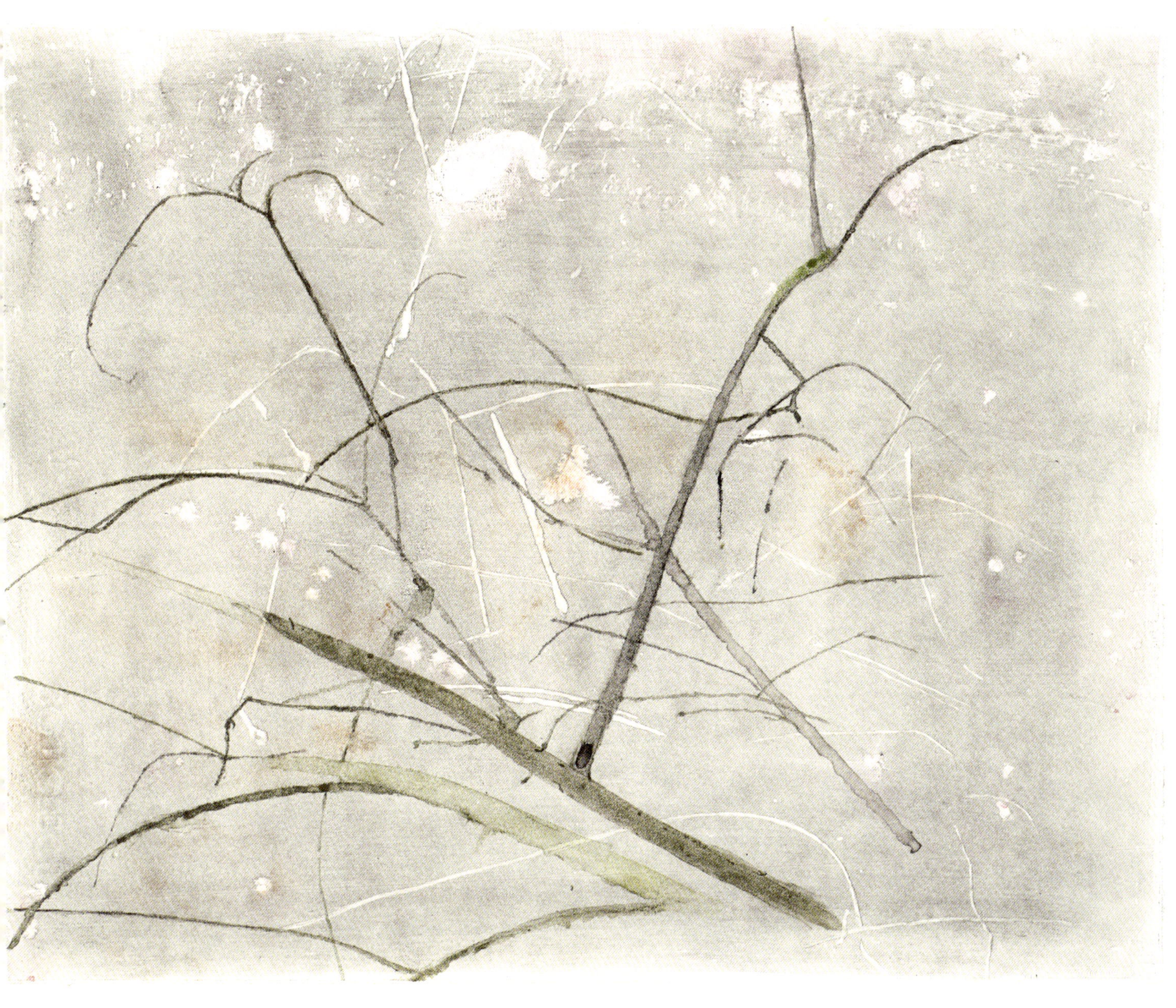

     CV15, 2020   watercolour monotype, 32.5 × 39.9 cm

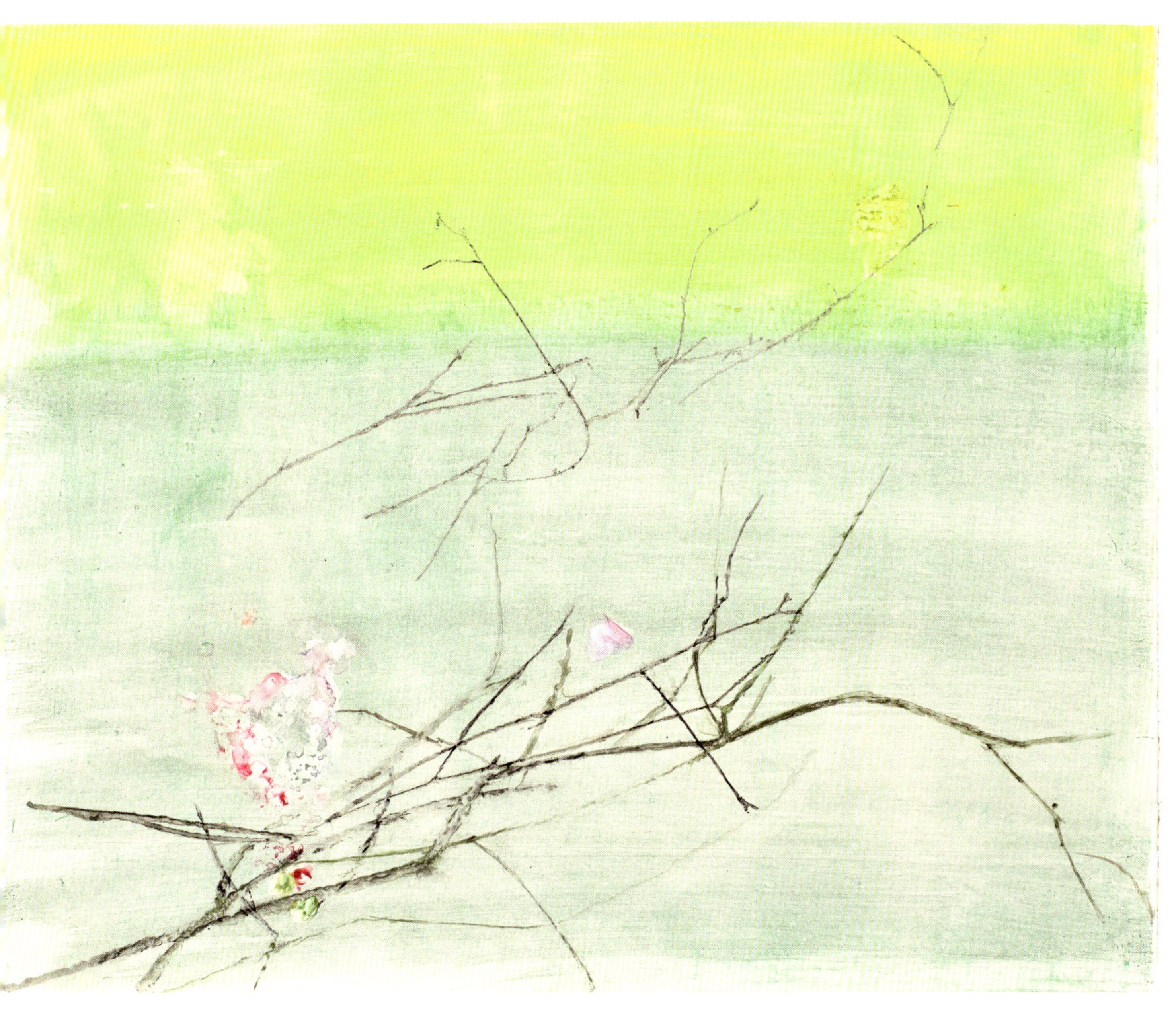

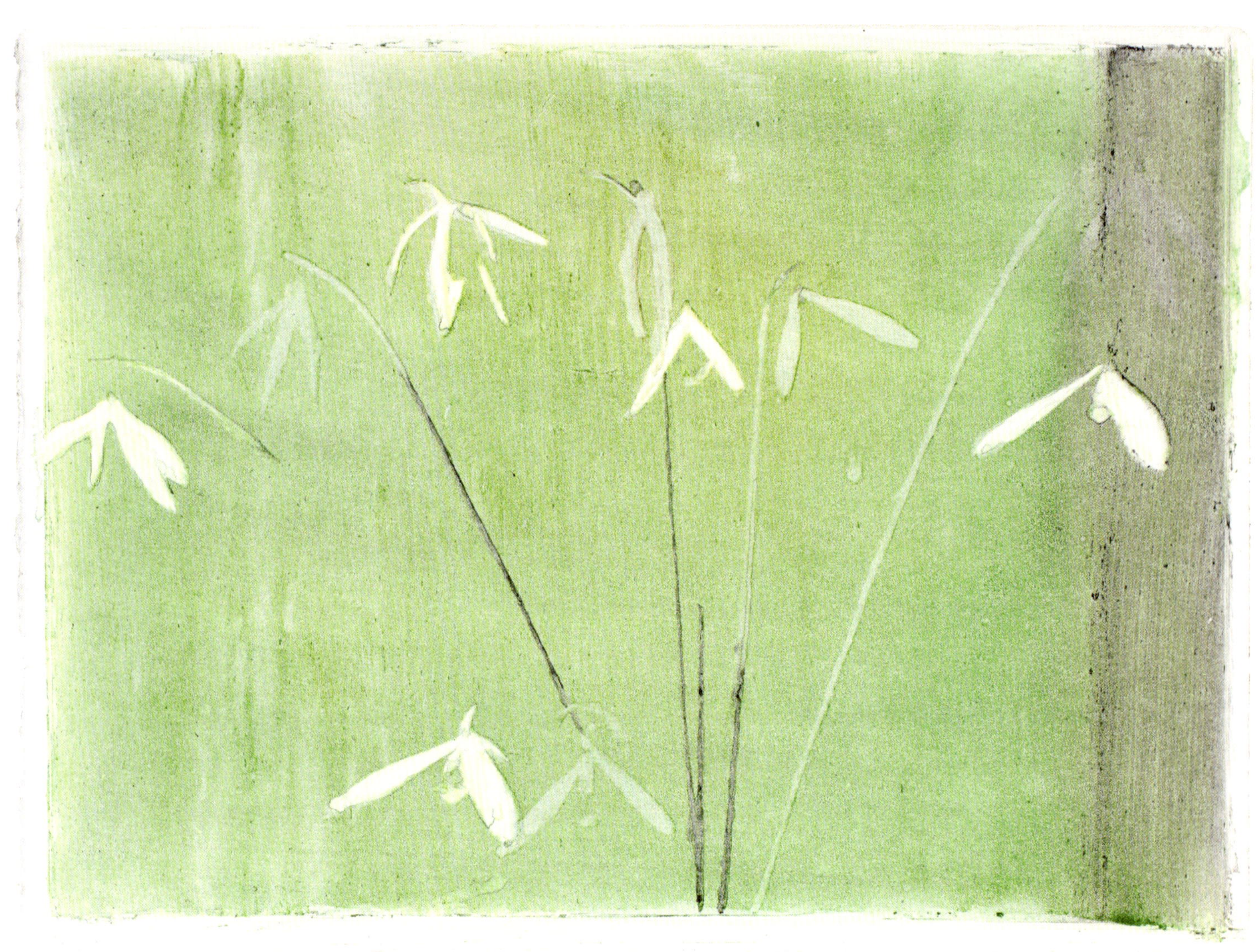

34   *CV16*, 2020   watercolour monotype, 20.8 × 28.6 cm

   CV19W, 2020   watercolour on watercolour monotype, 32.8 × 40.1 cm

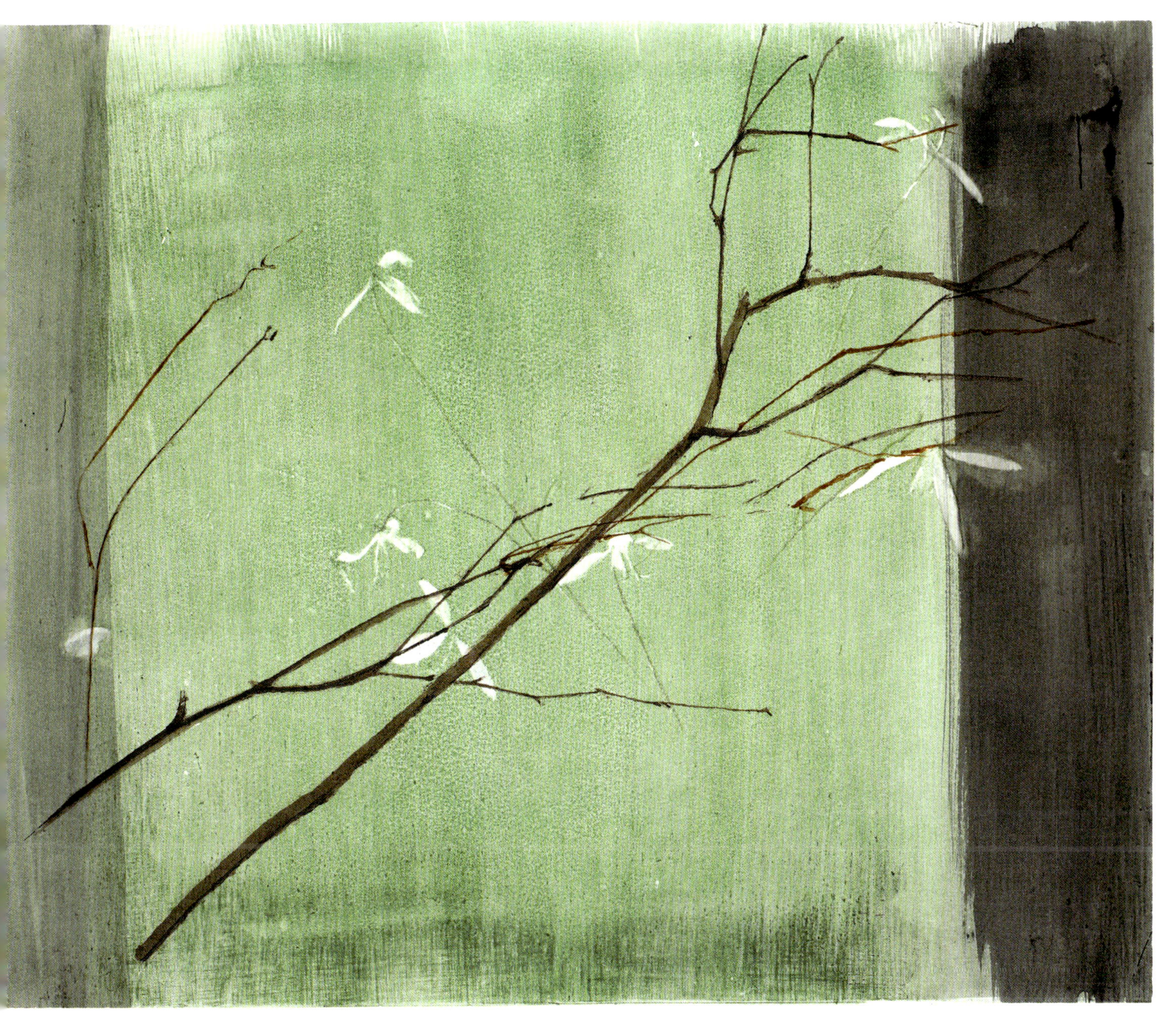

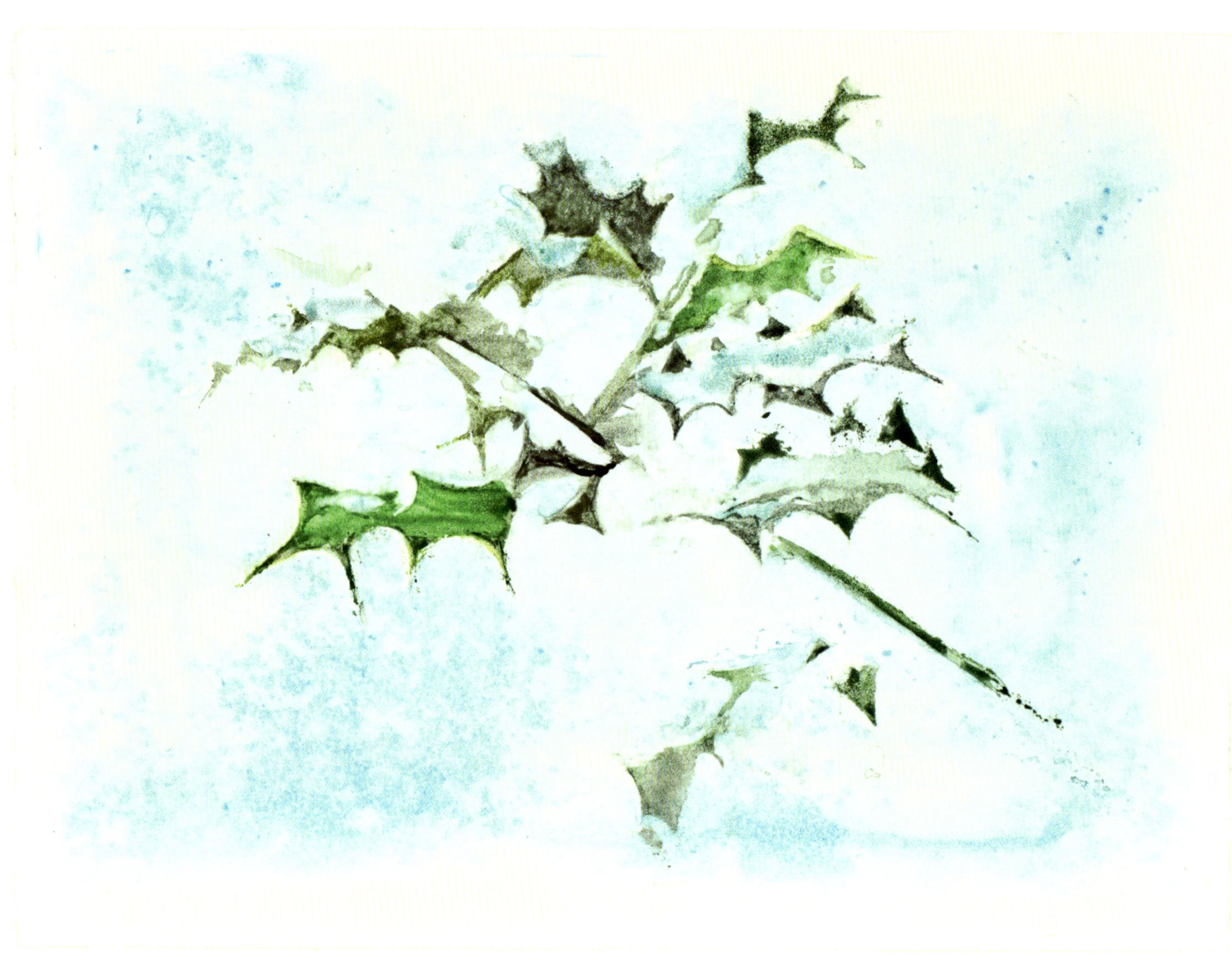

  CV21, 2020   watercolour monotype, 21 × 28.8 cm

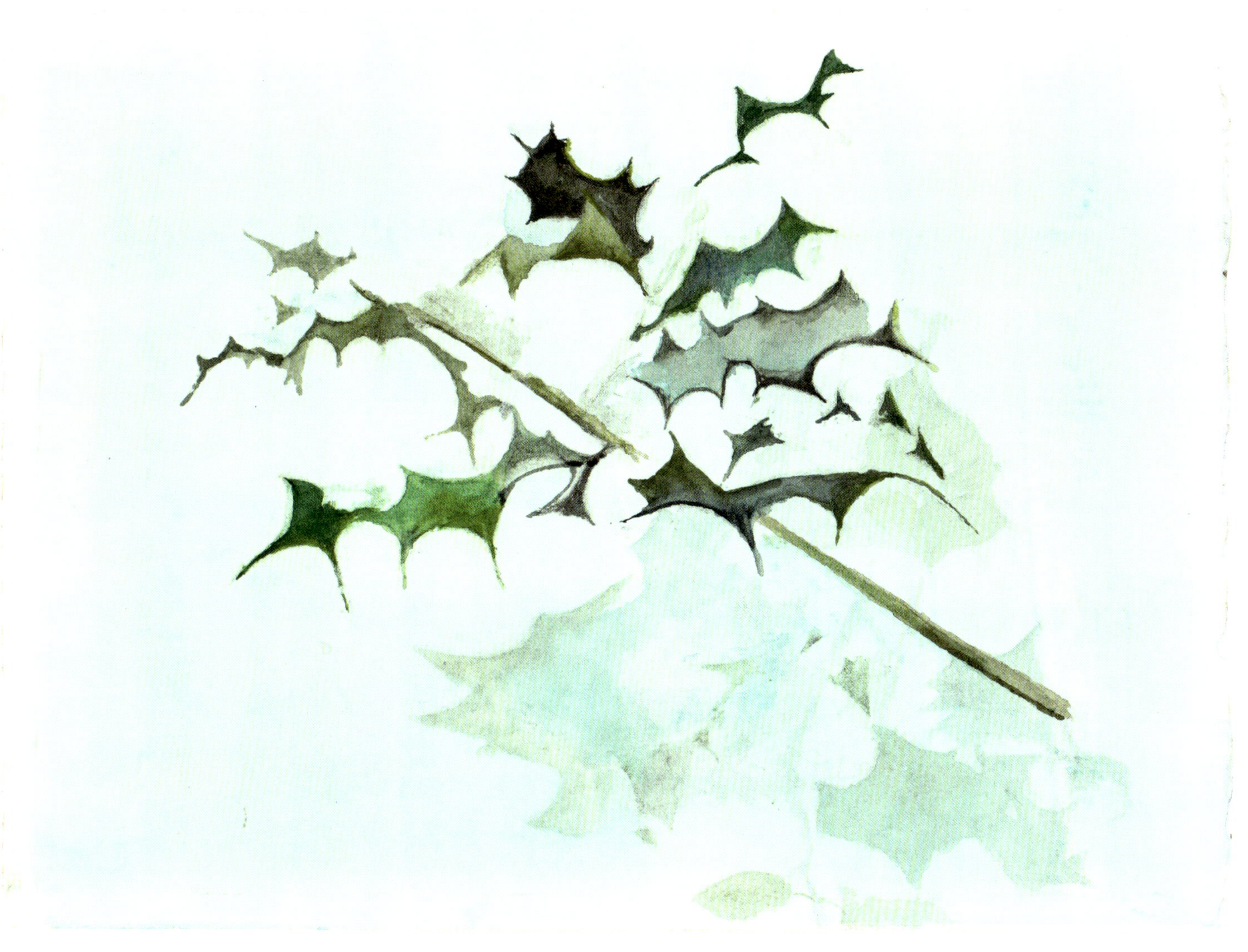

CV20W, 2020–21   watercolour on watercolour monotype, 20.7 × 28.6 cm   39

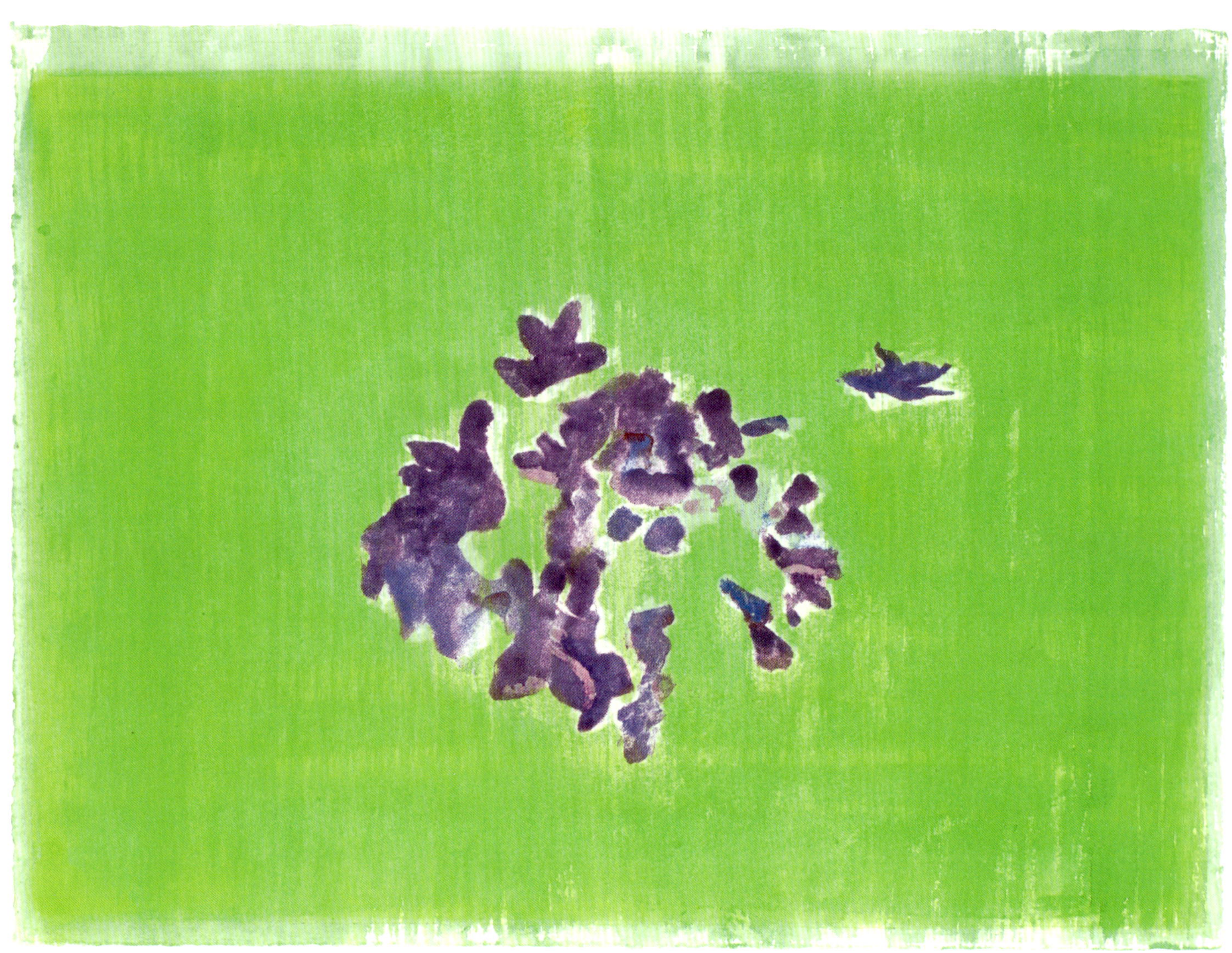

40   *CV22W*, 2020–21   watercolour on watercolour monotype, 21.1 × 28.7 cm

   CV25, 2020   watercolour monotype, 32.7 × 41 cm

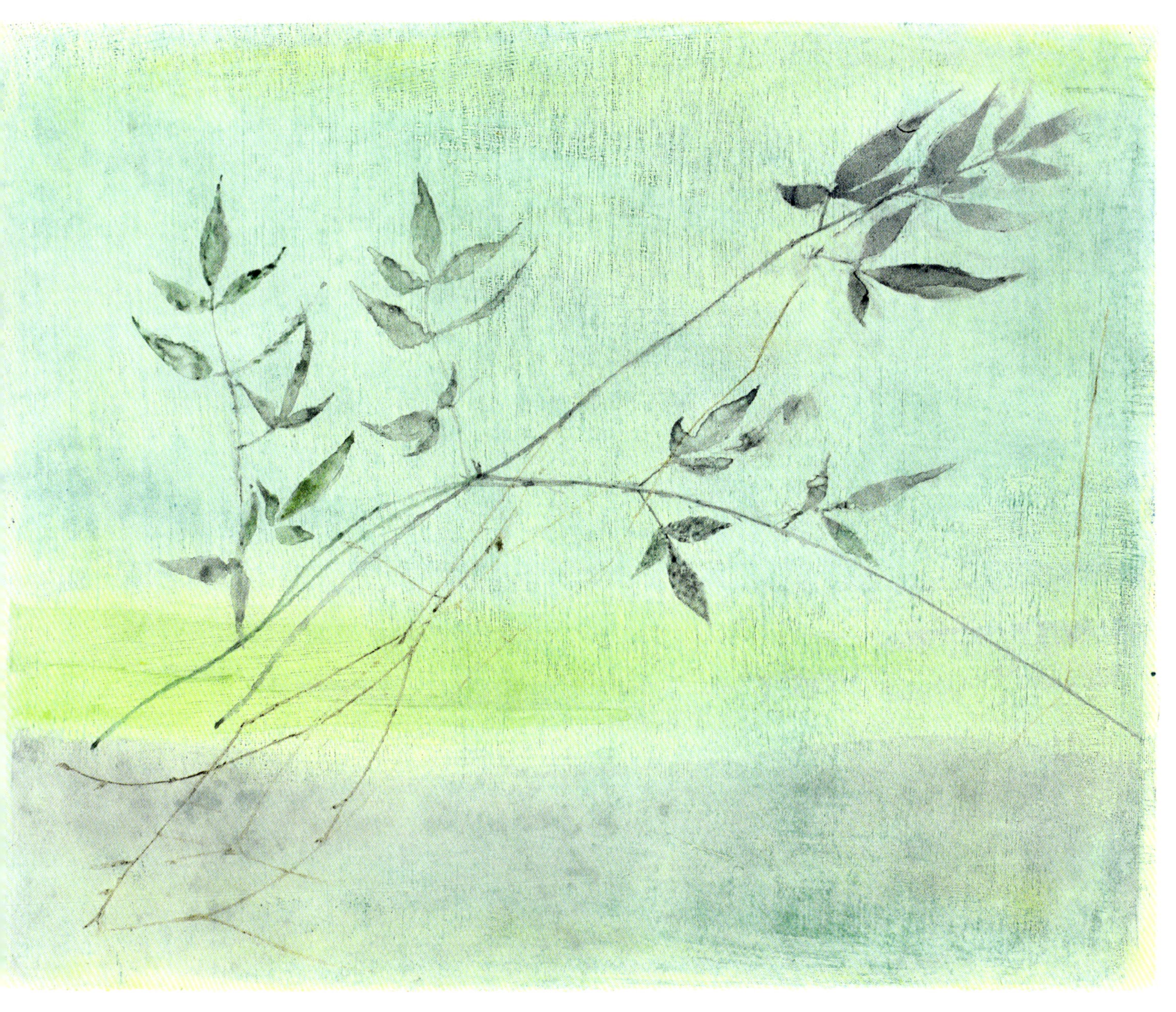

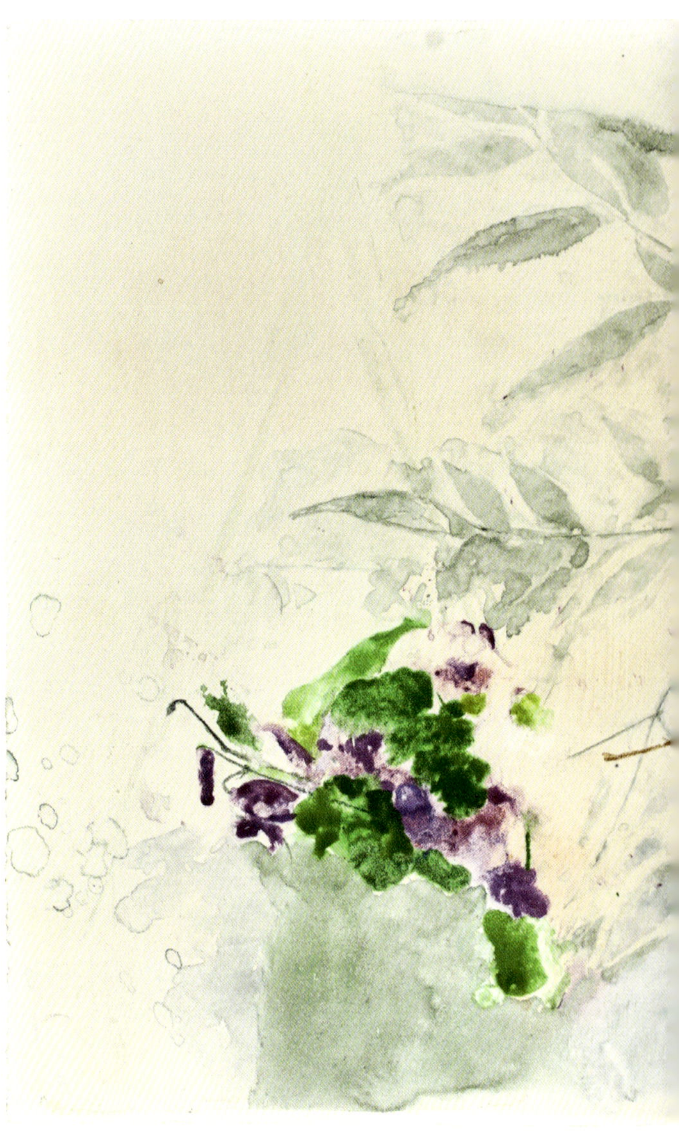

44   *CV26*, 2020   watercolour monotype, 28.2 × 61.3 cm

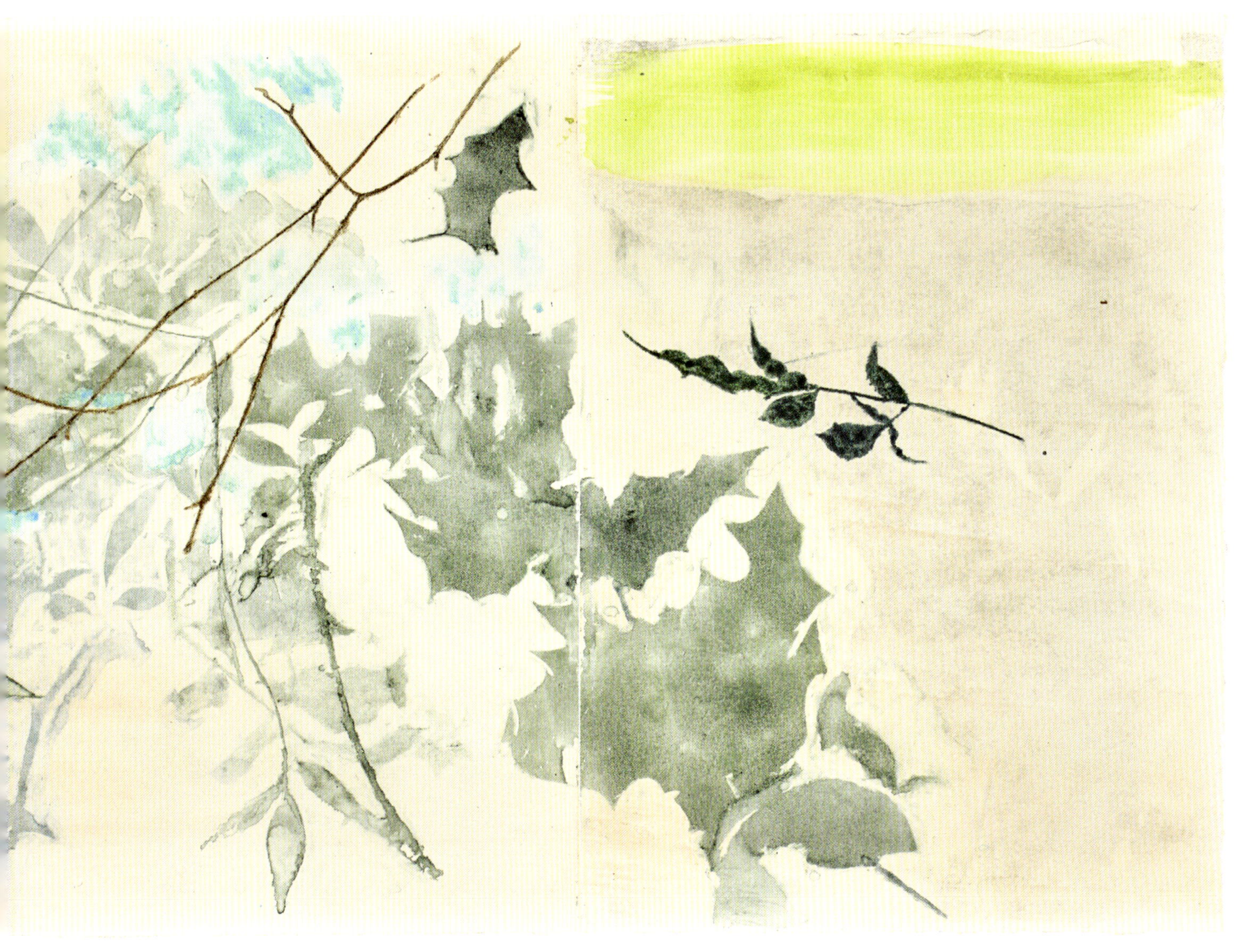

    CV27, 2020   watercolour monotype, 32.8 × 40.8 cm

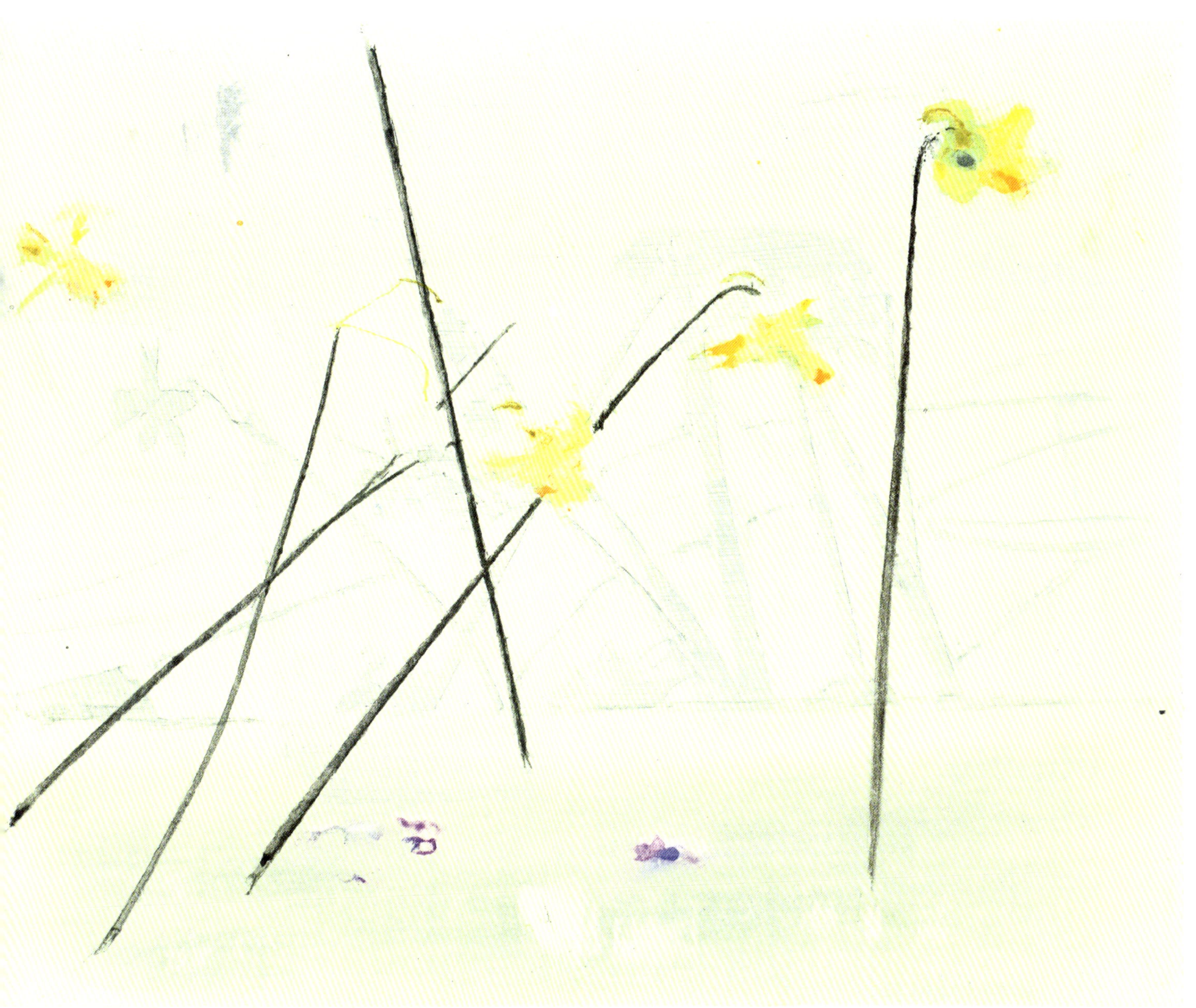

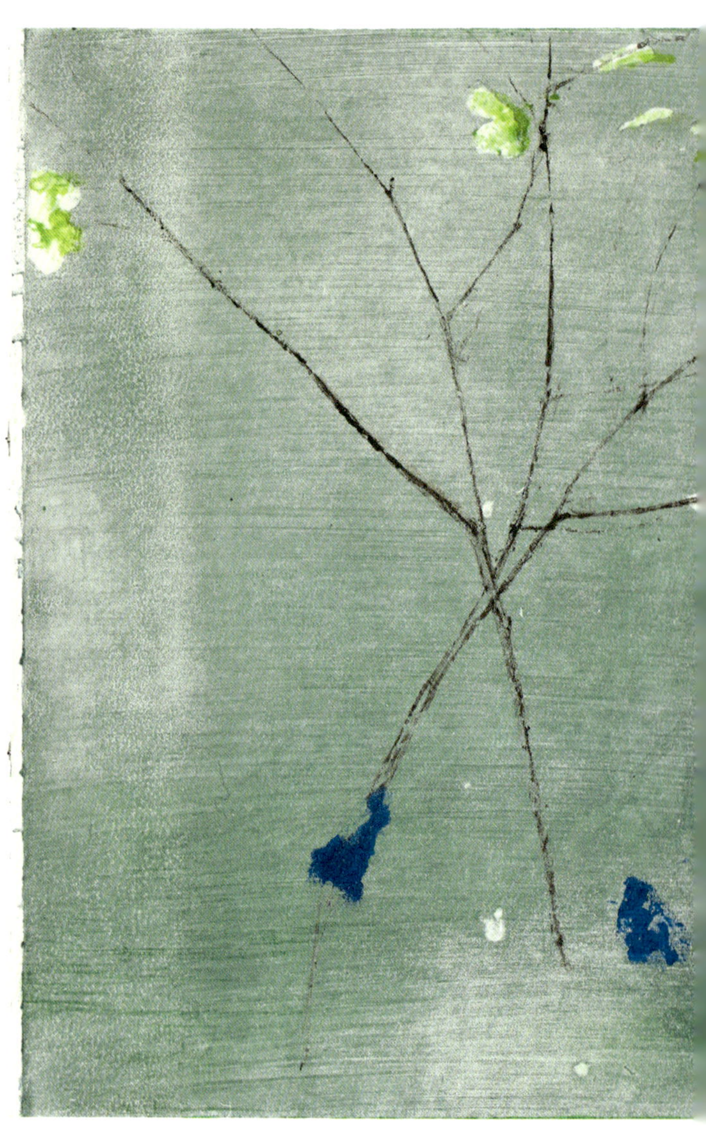

48   *CV28*, 2020   watercolour monotype, 27.6 × 61.6 cm

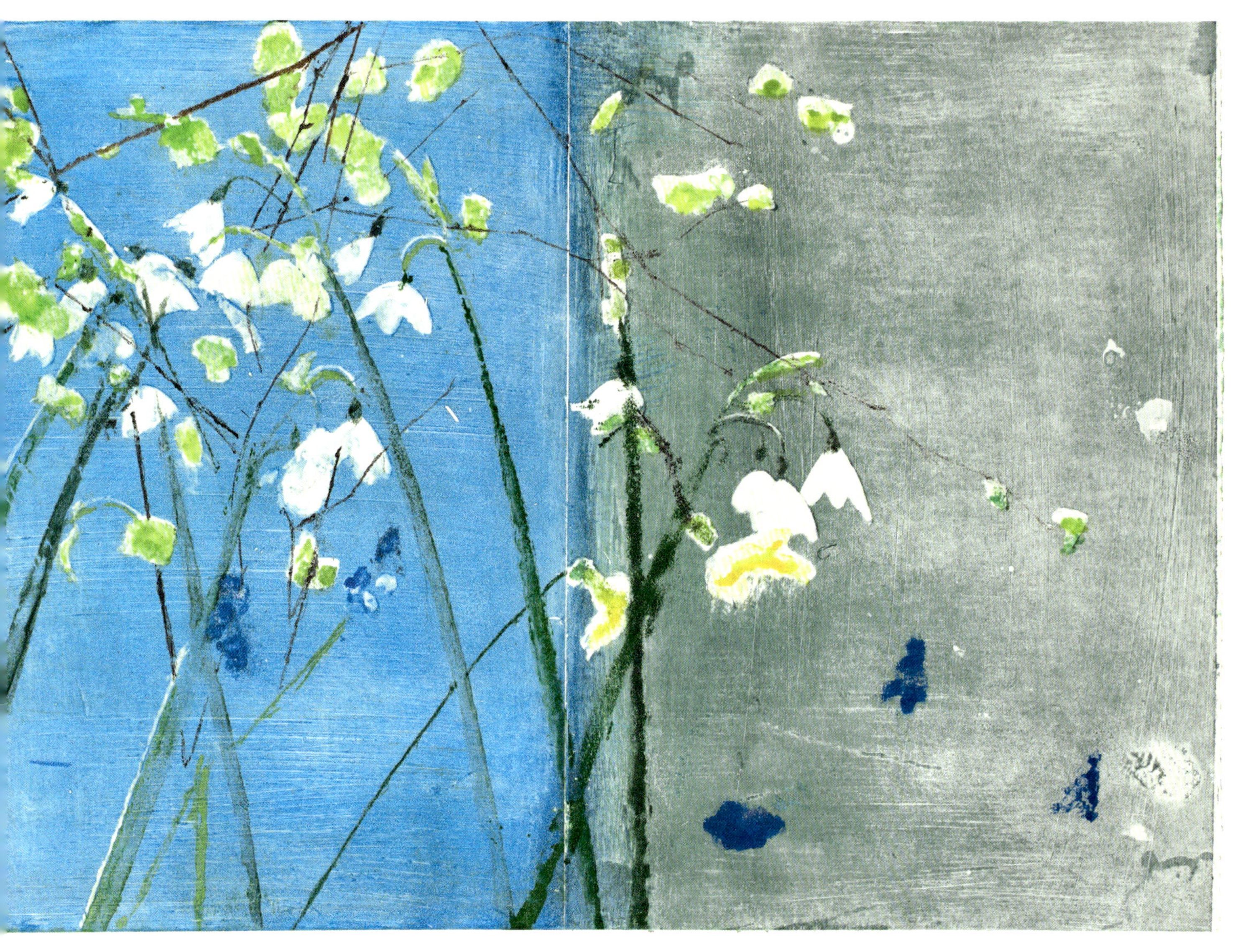

    CV29W, 2020–21   watercolour on watercolour monotype, 27.9 × 40.2 cm

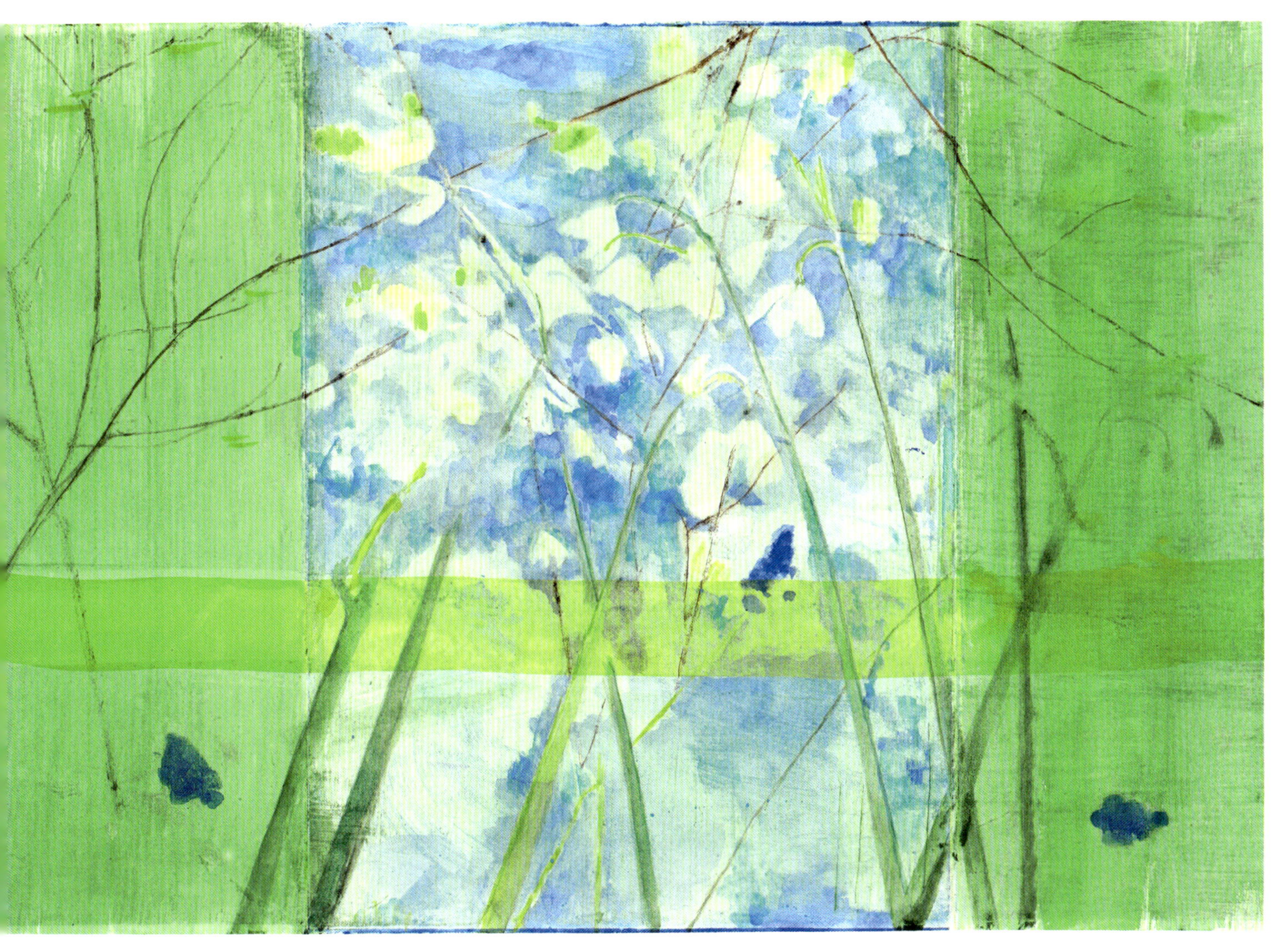

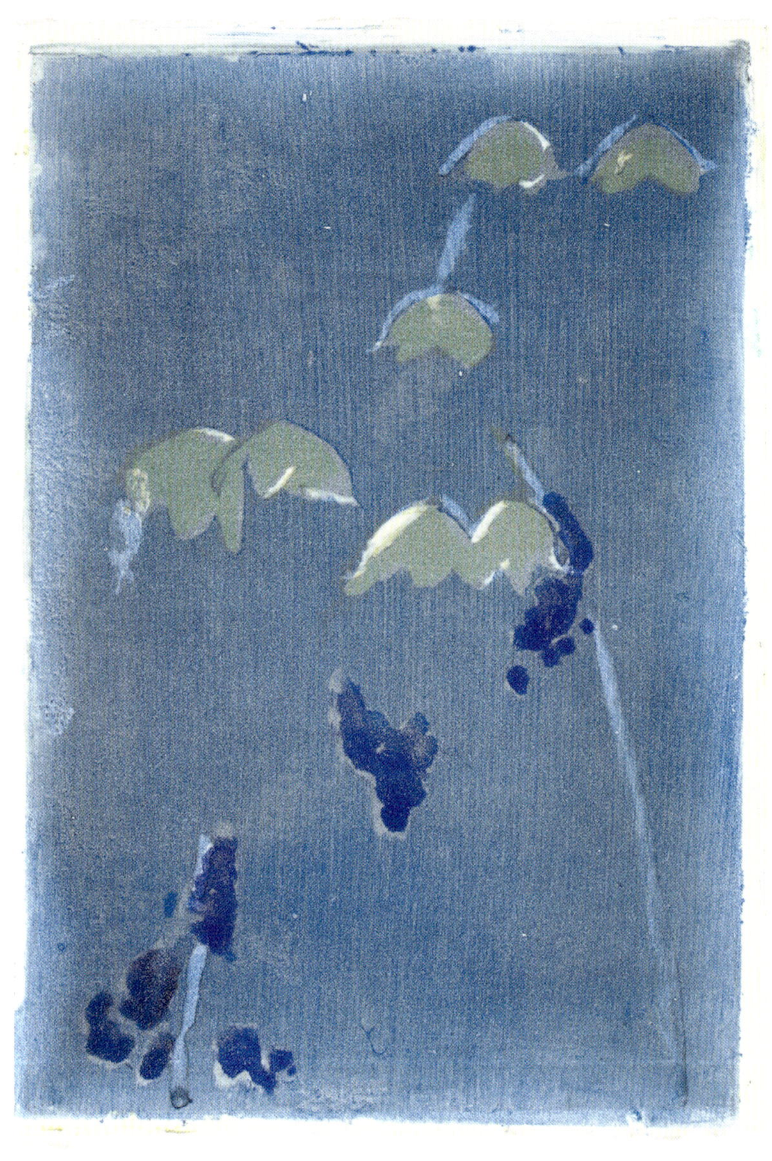

   CV30, 2020   watercolour monotype, 20.7 × 14.5 cm

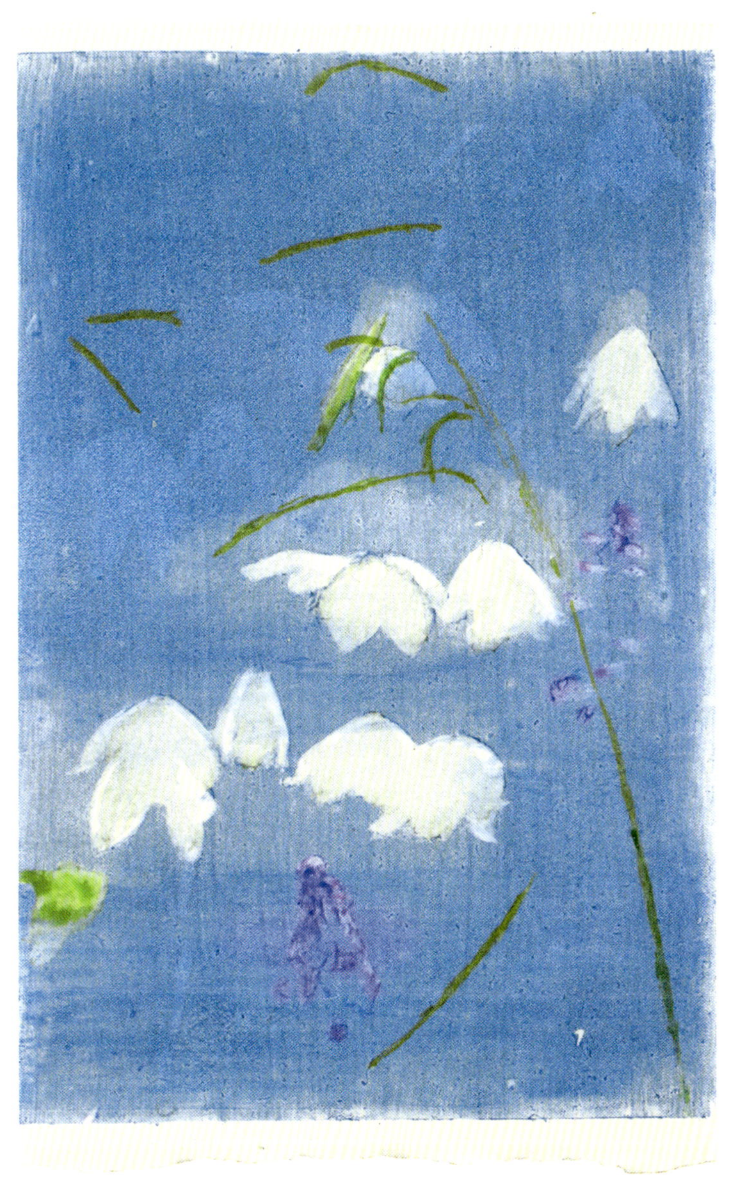

CV31, 2020   watercolour monotype, 21.5 × 13.4 cm   53

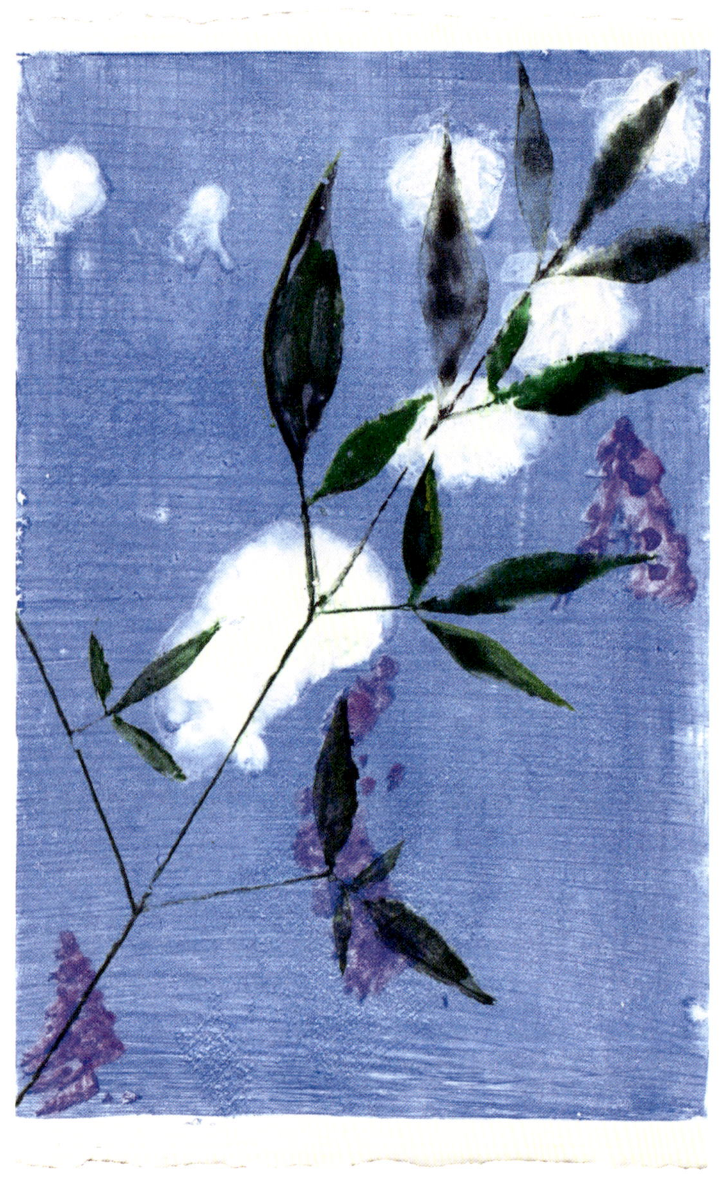

54   *CV32*, 2020   watercolour monotype, 21.5 × 13.5 cm

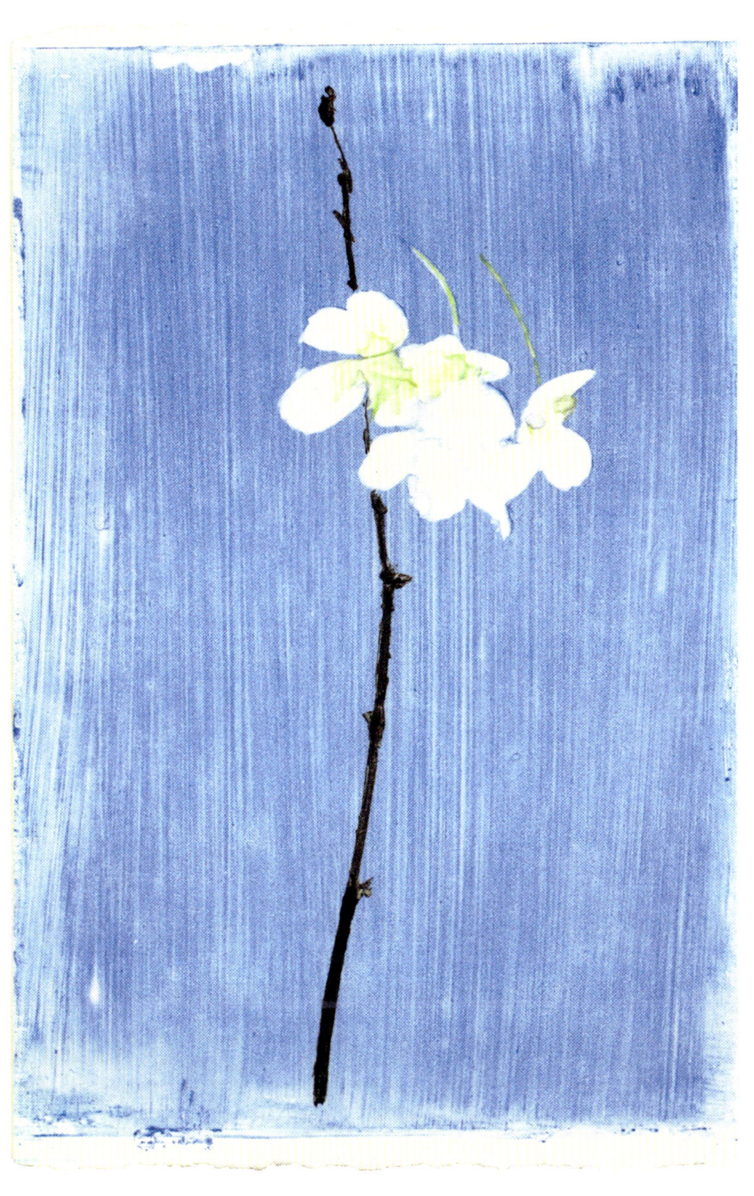

CV33, 2020   watercolour monotype, 21.3 × 14 cm

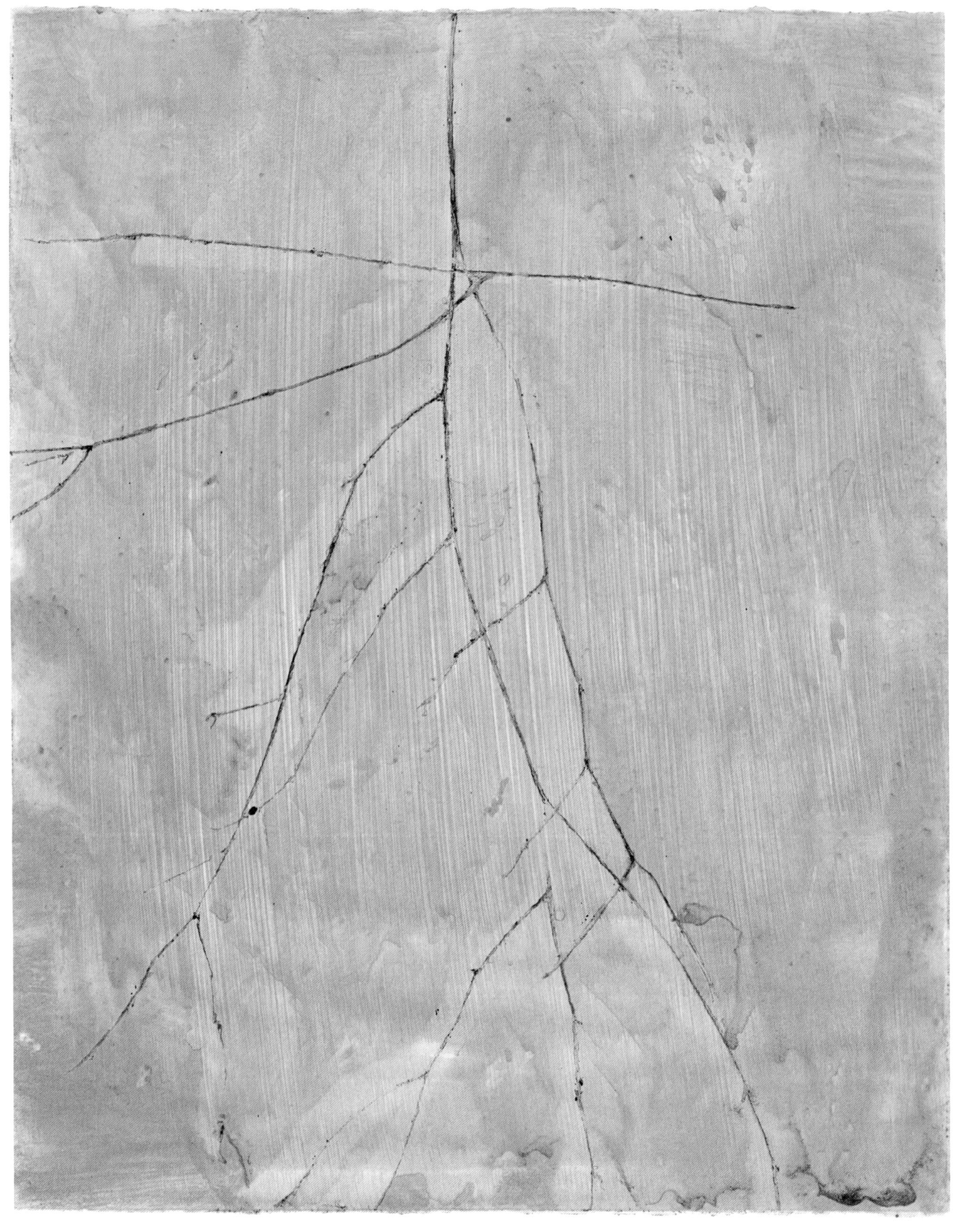

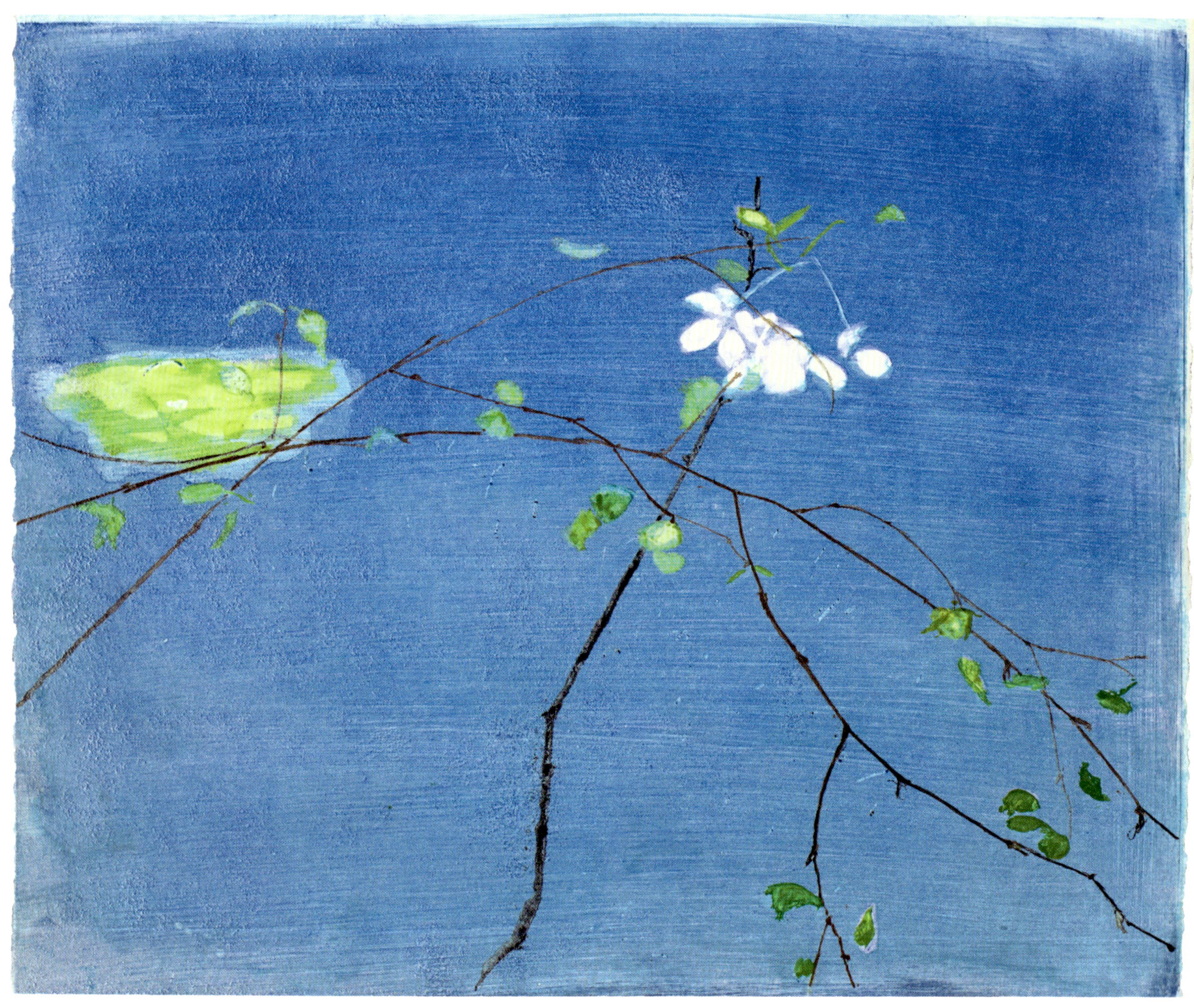

58   *CV36*, 2020   watercolour monotype, 32.6 × 40.7 cm

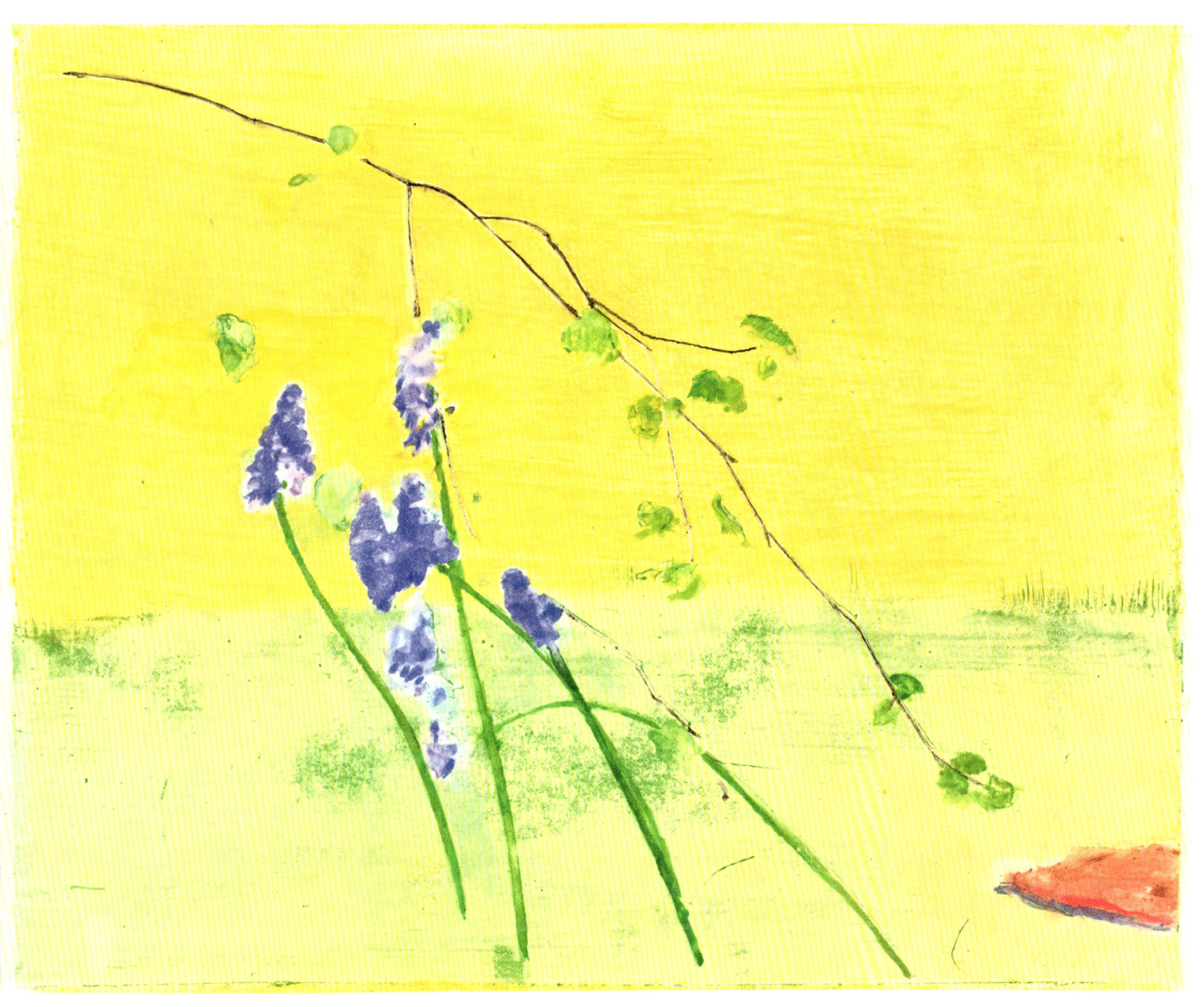

    CV38, 2020   watercolour monotype, 19.3 × 27.4 cm

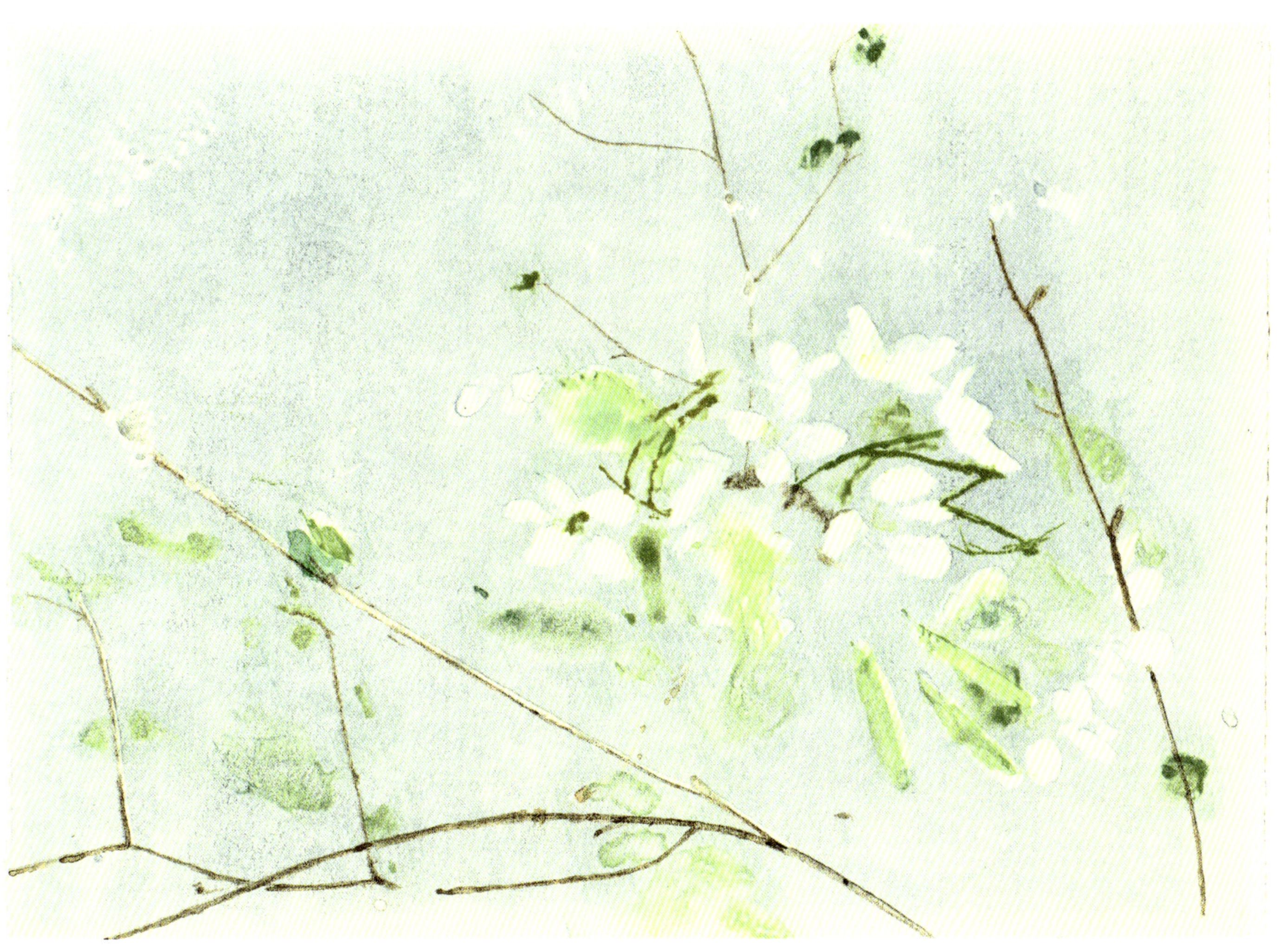

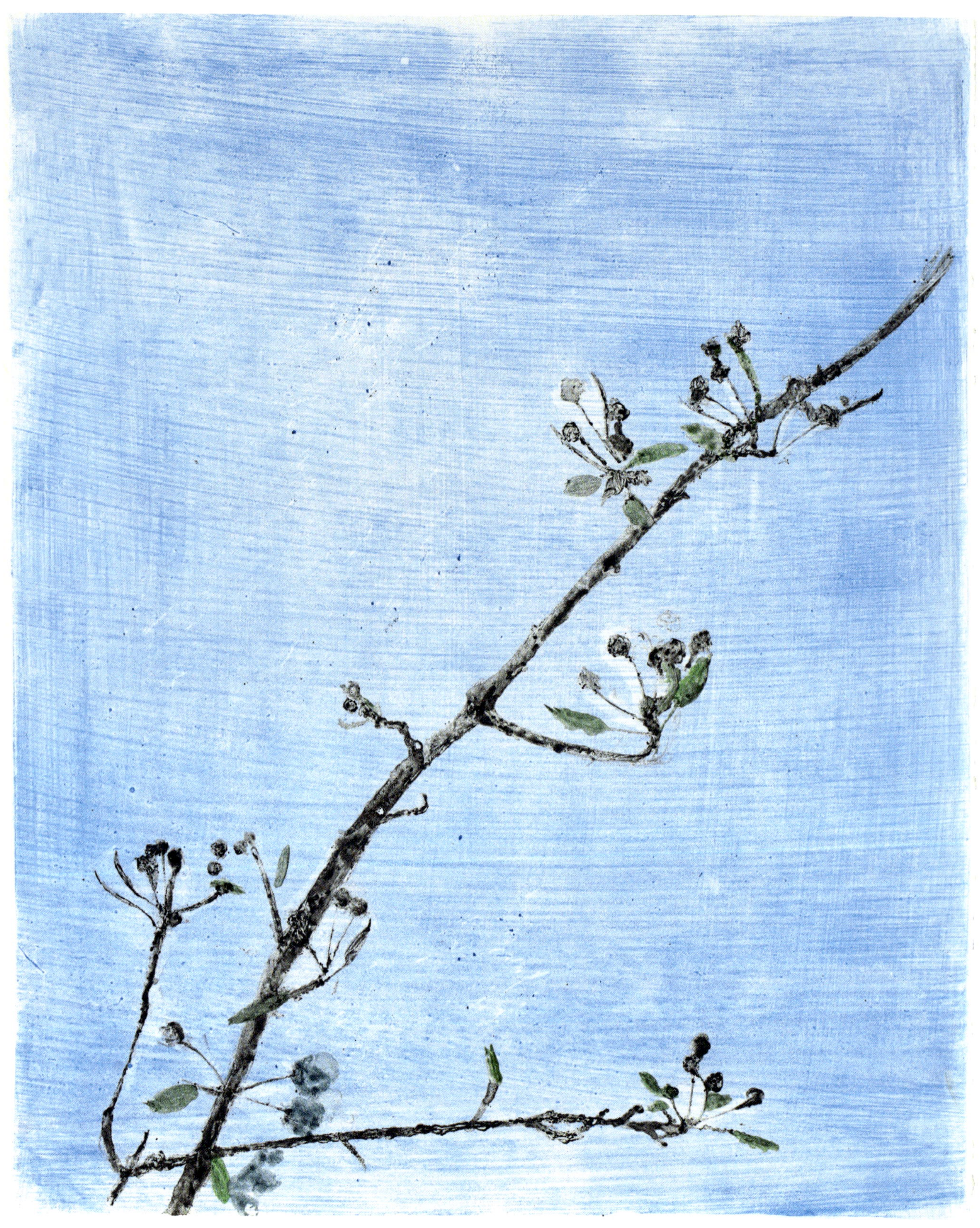

  CV39, 2020   watercolour monotype, 40.1 × 33.3 cm

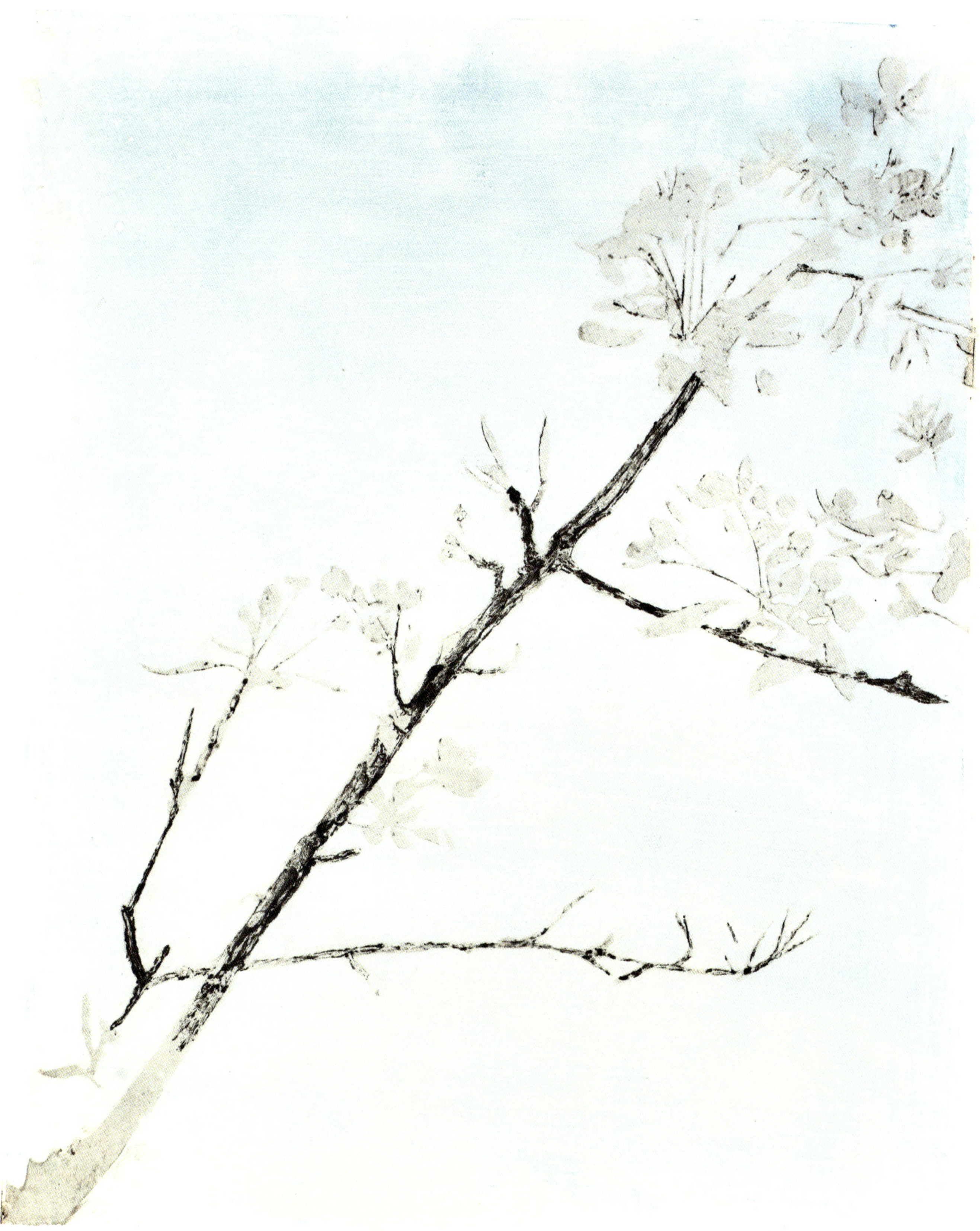

CV40, 2020   watercolour monotype, 40.2 × 33.4 cm   63

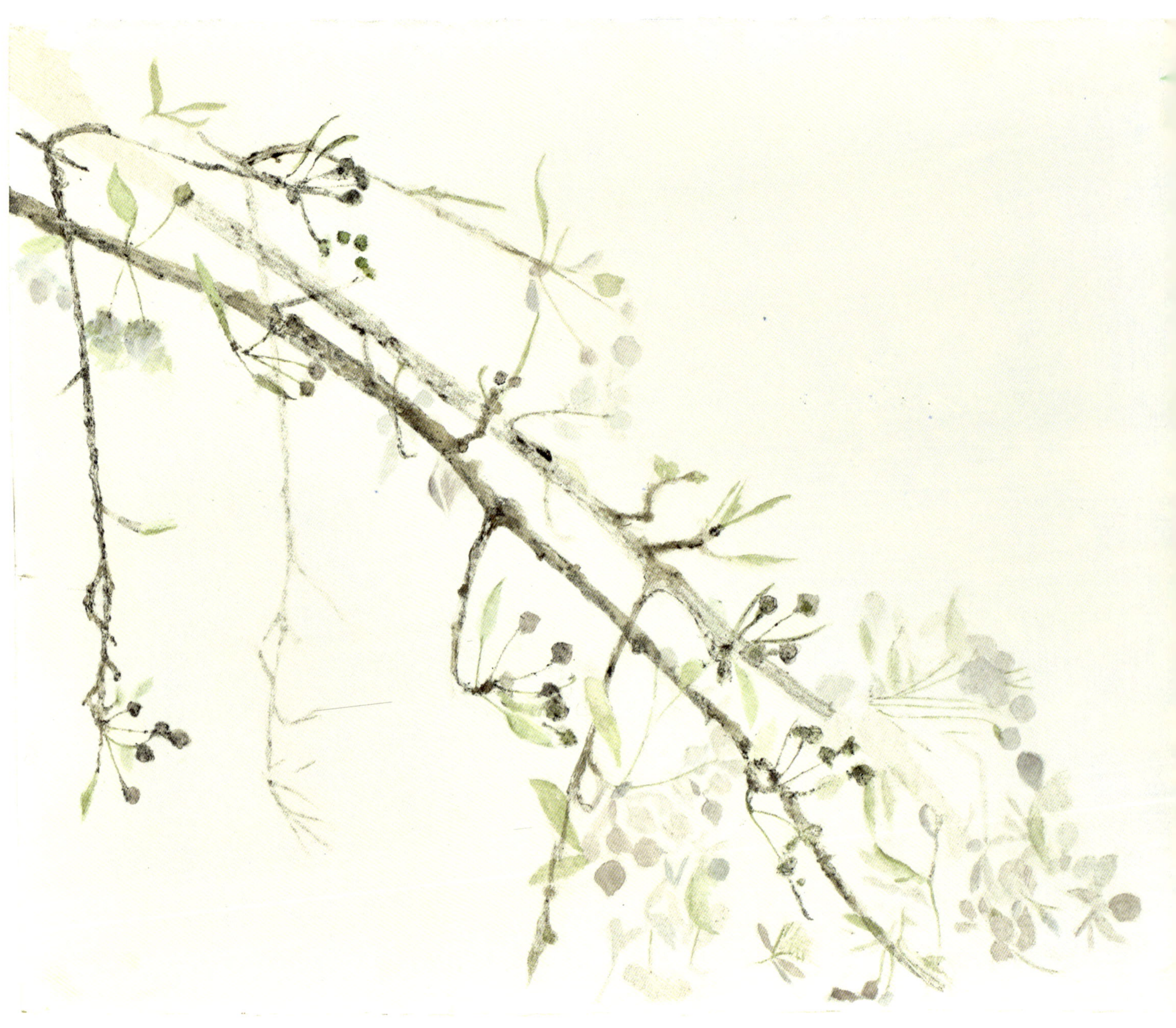

64   *CV41W*, 2020–21   watercolour on watercolour monotype, 33.4 × 40.1 cm

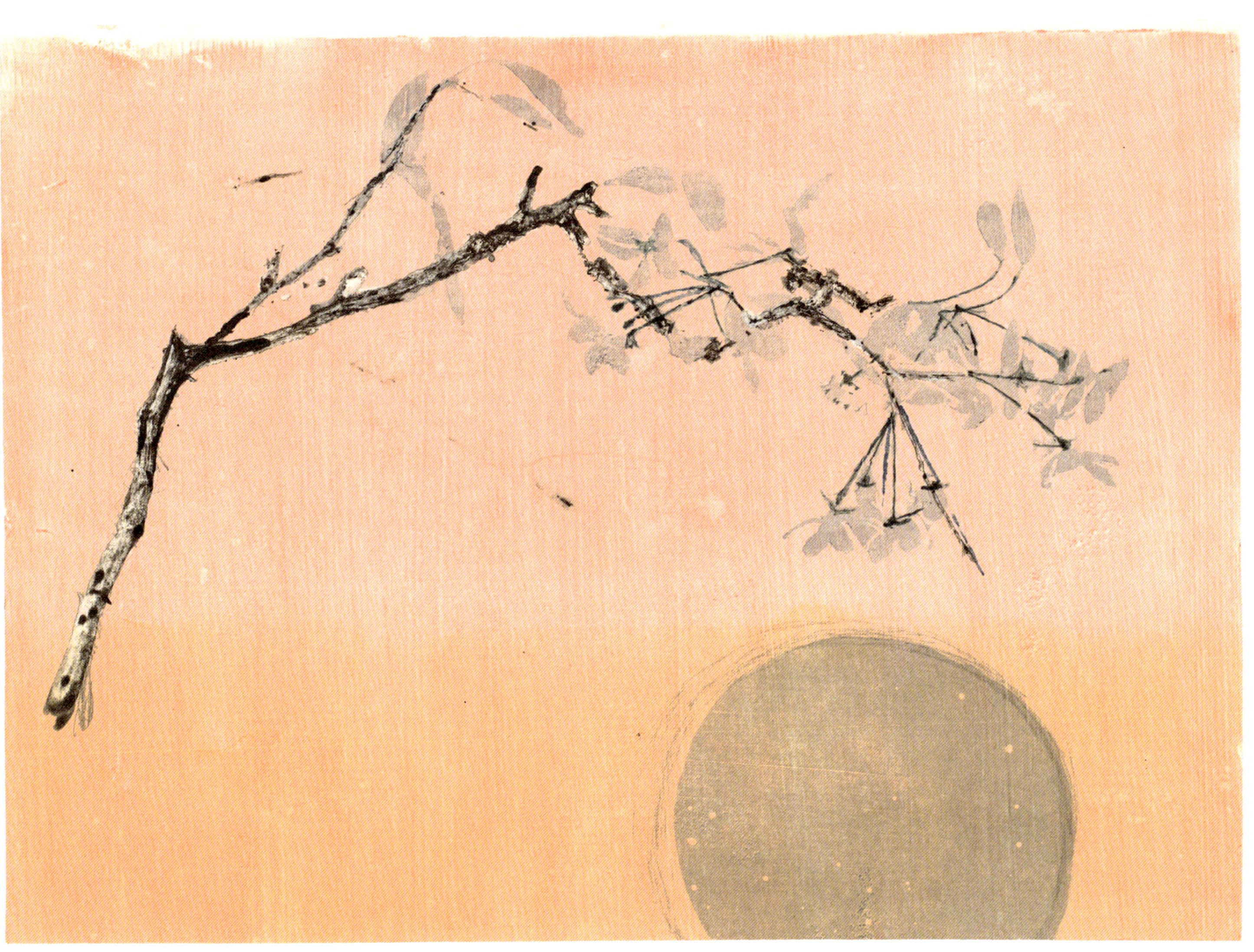

CV42W, 2020–21   watercolour on watercolour monotype, 28.1 × 39.2 cm   65

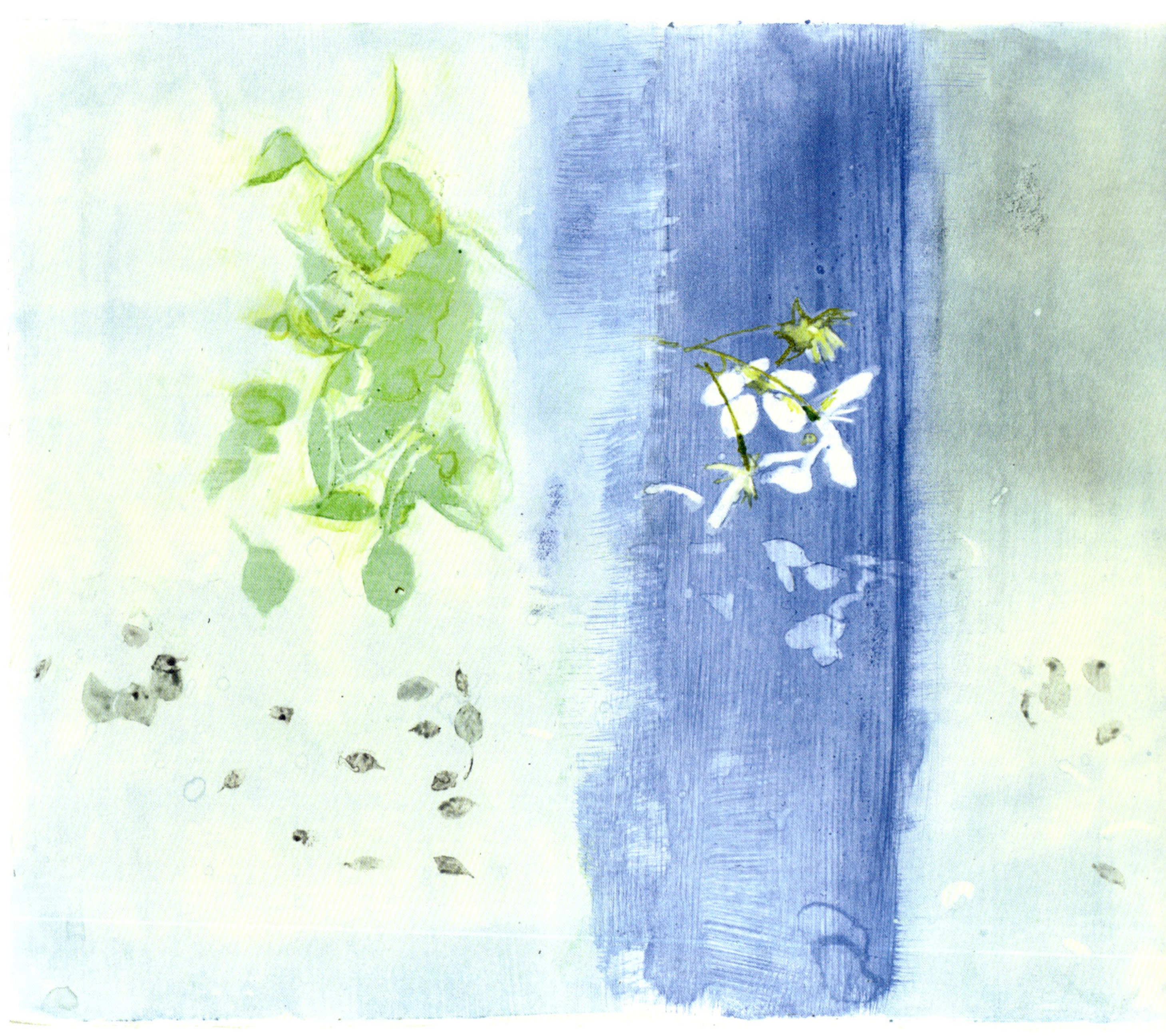

   CV43, 2020   watercolour monotype, 33.3 × 40.2 cm

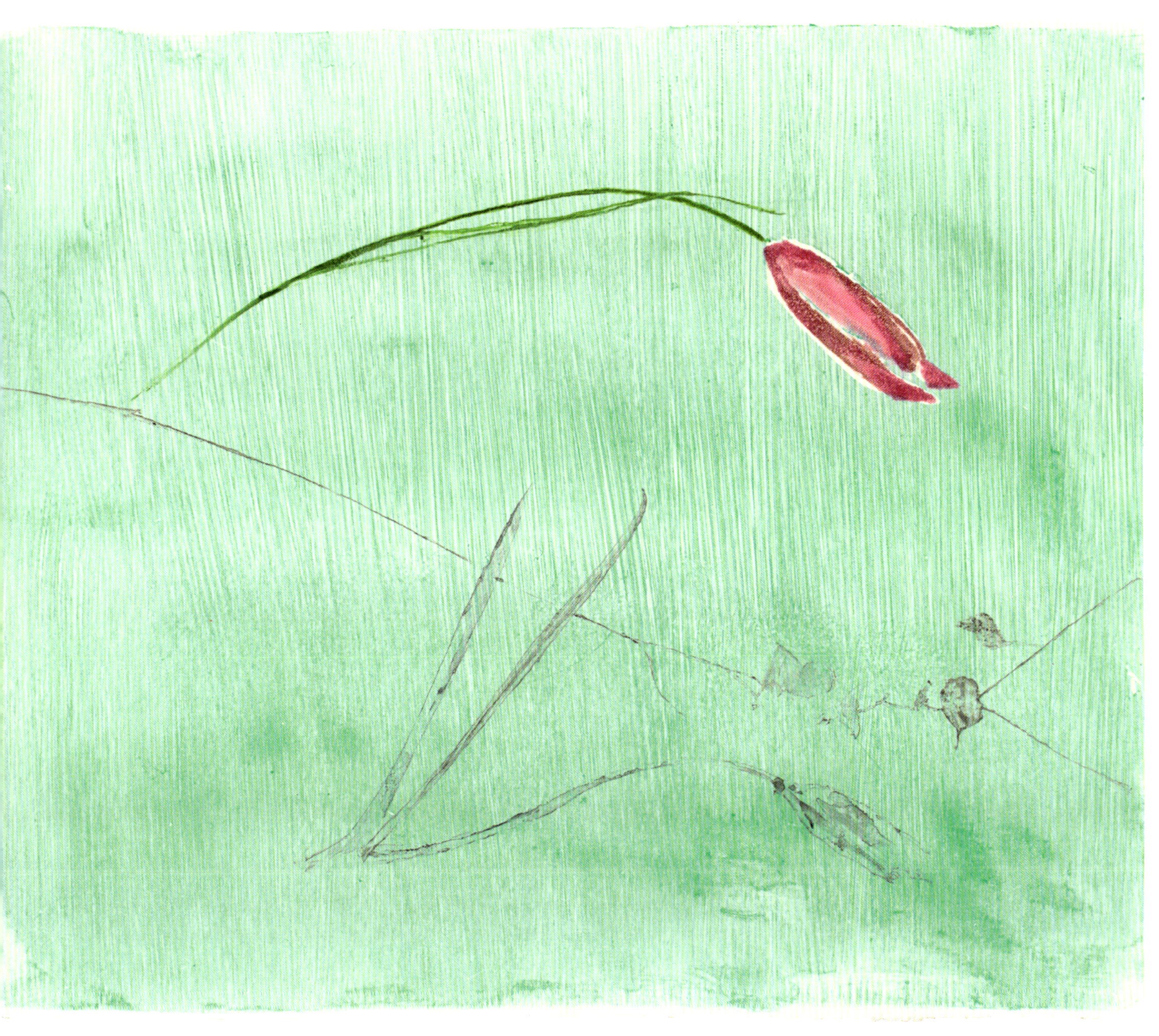

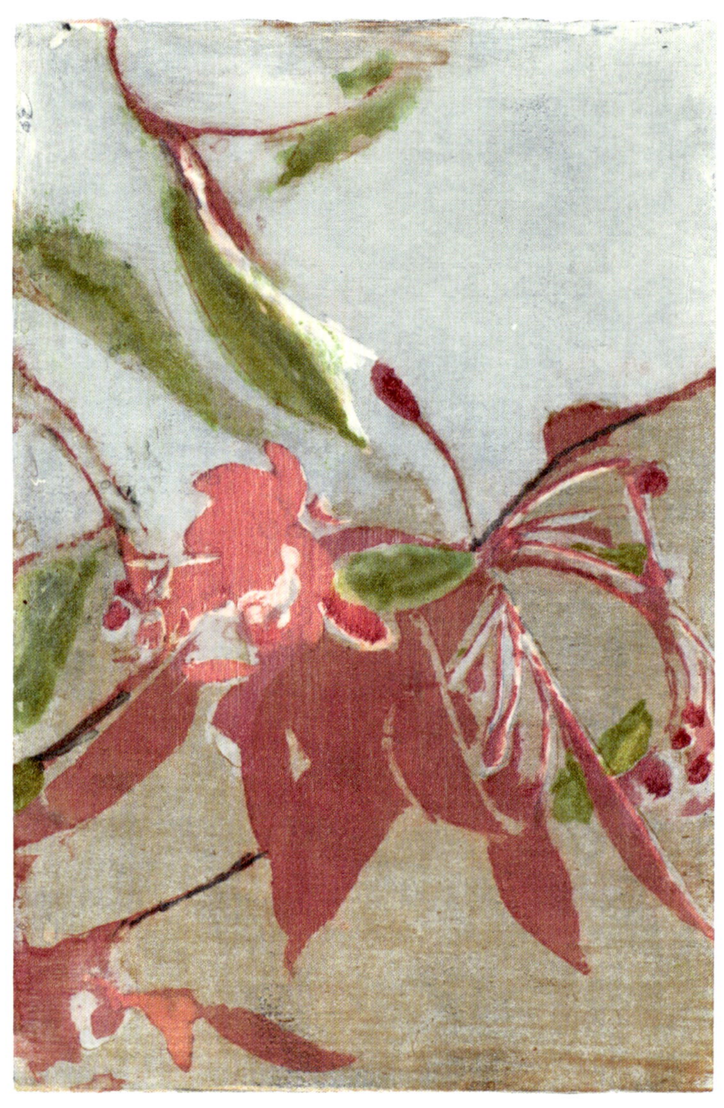

    CV45, 2020   watercolour monotype, 19.8 × 13.5 cm

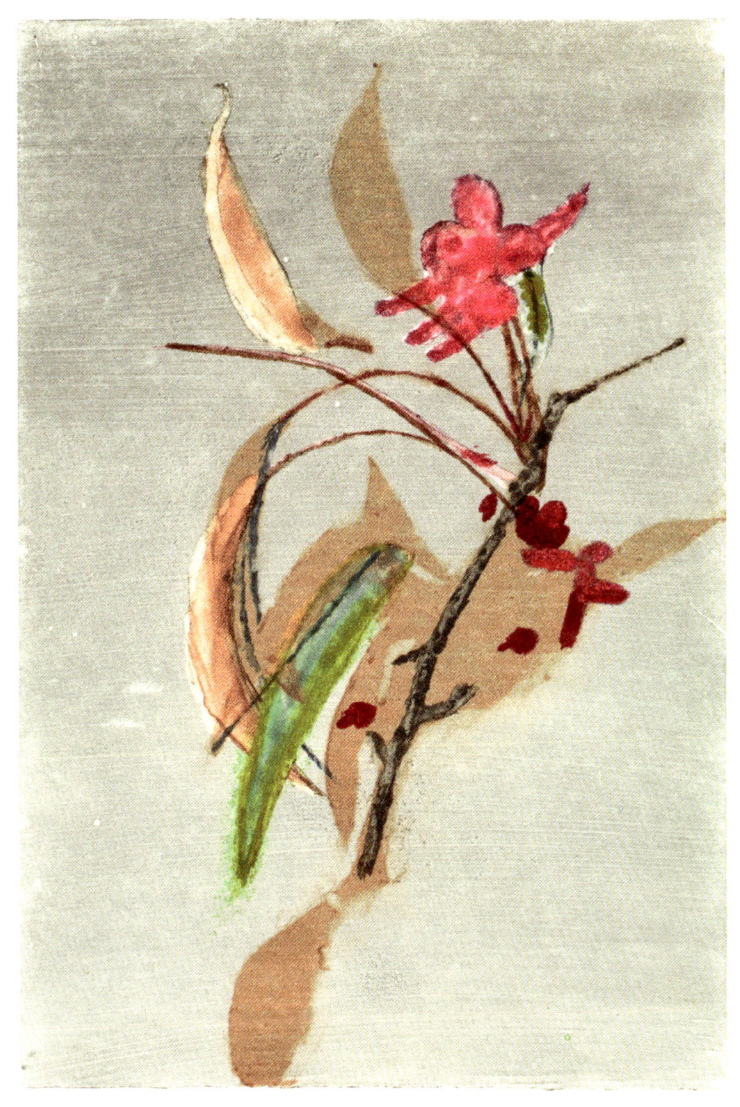

    CV48, 2020   watercolour monotype, 27.6 × 50.2 cm

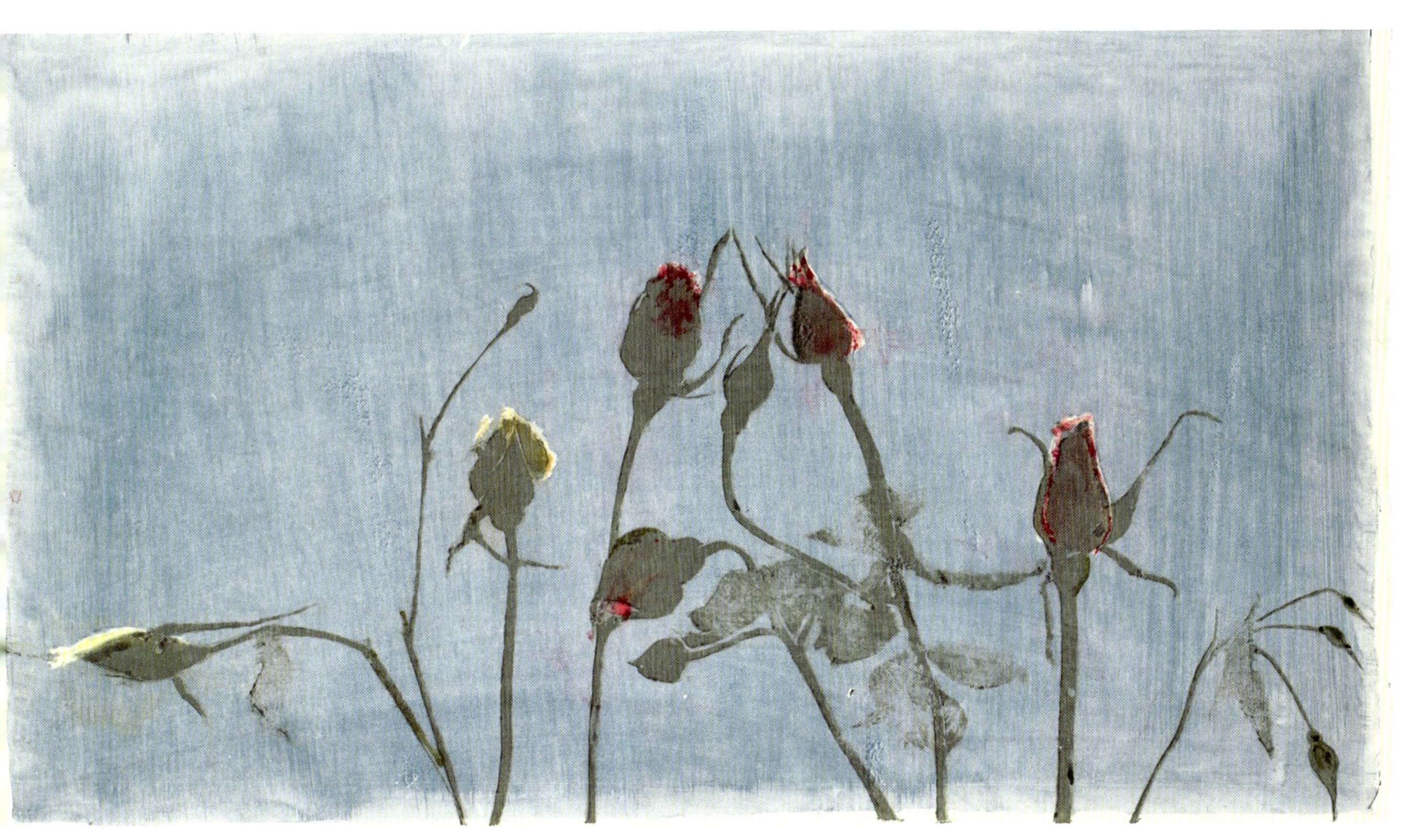

    CV49, 2020   watercolour monotype, 27.8 × 50.4 cm

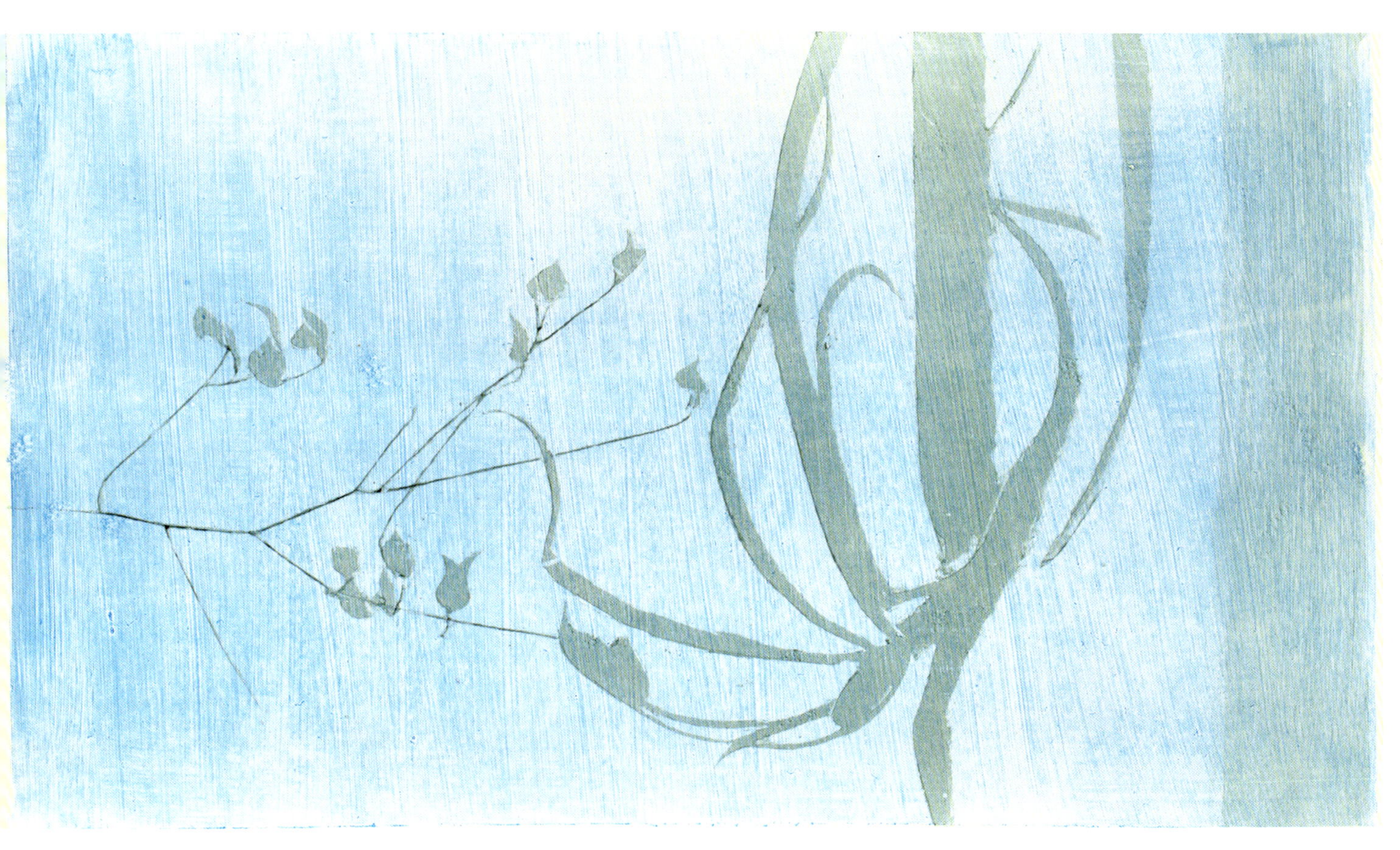

    CV50, 2020   watercolour monotype, 19.3 × 28.4 cm

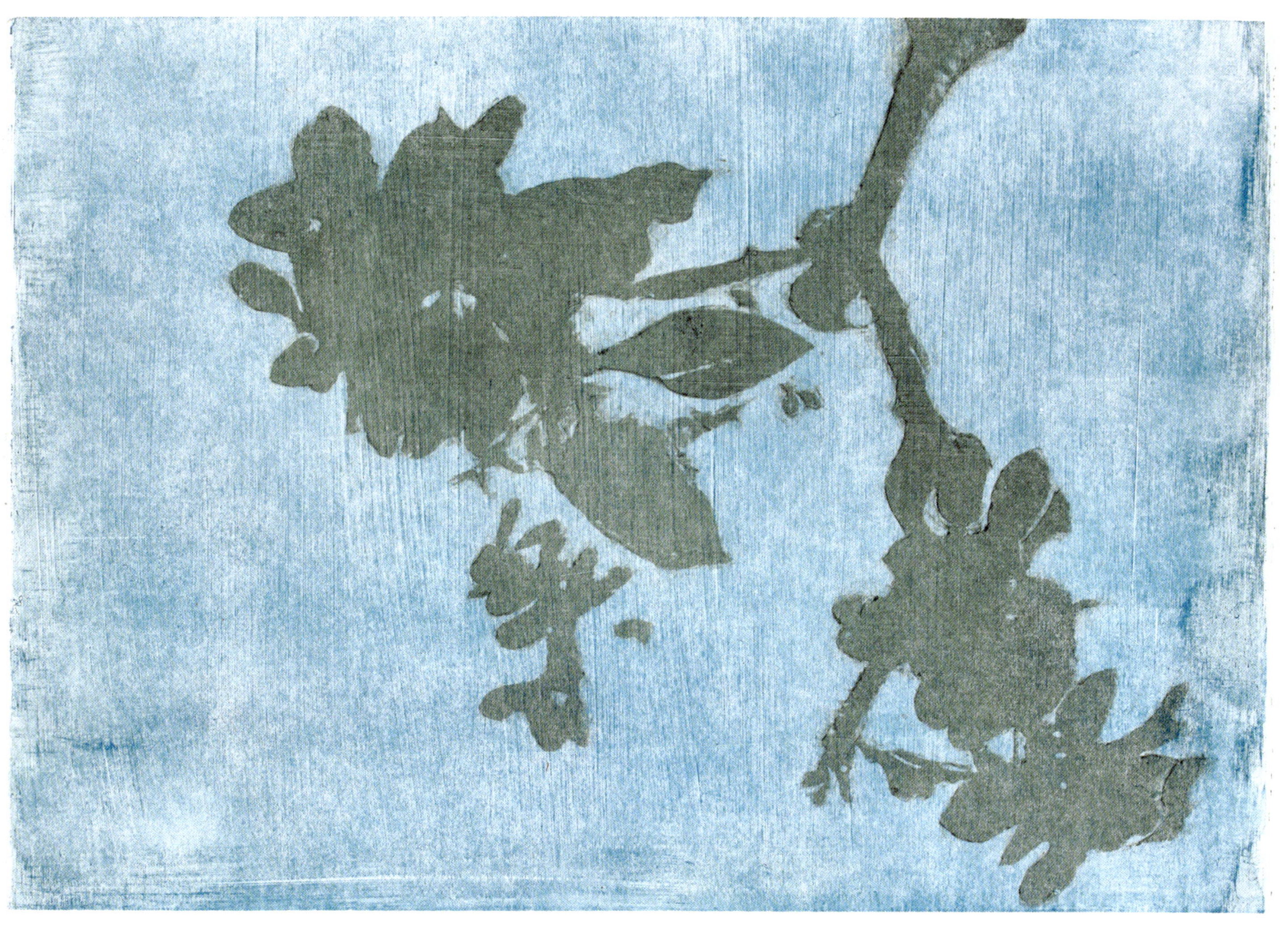

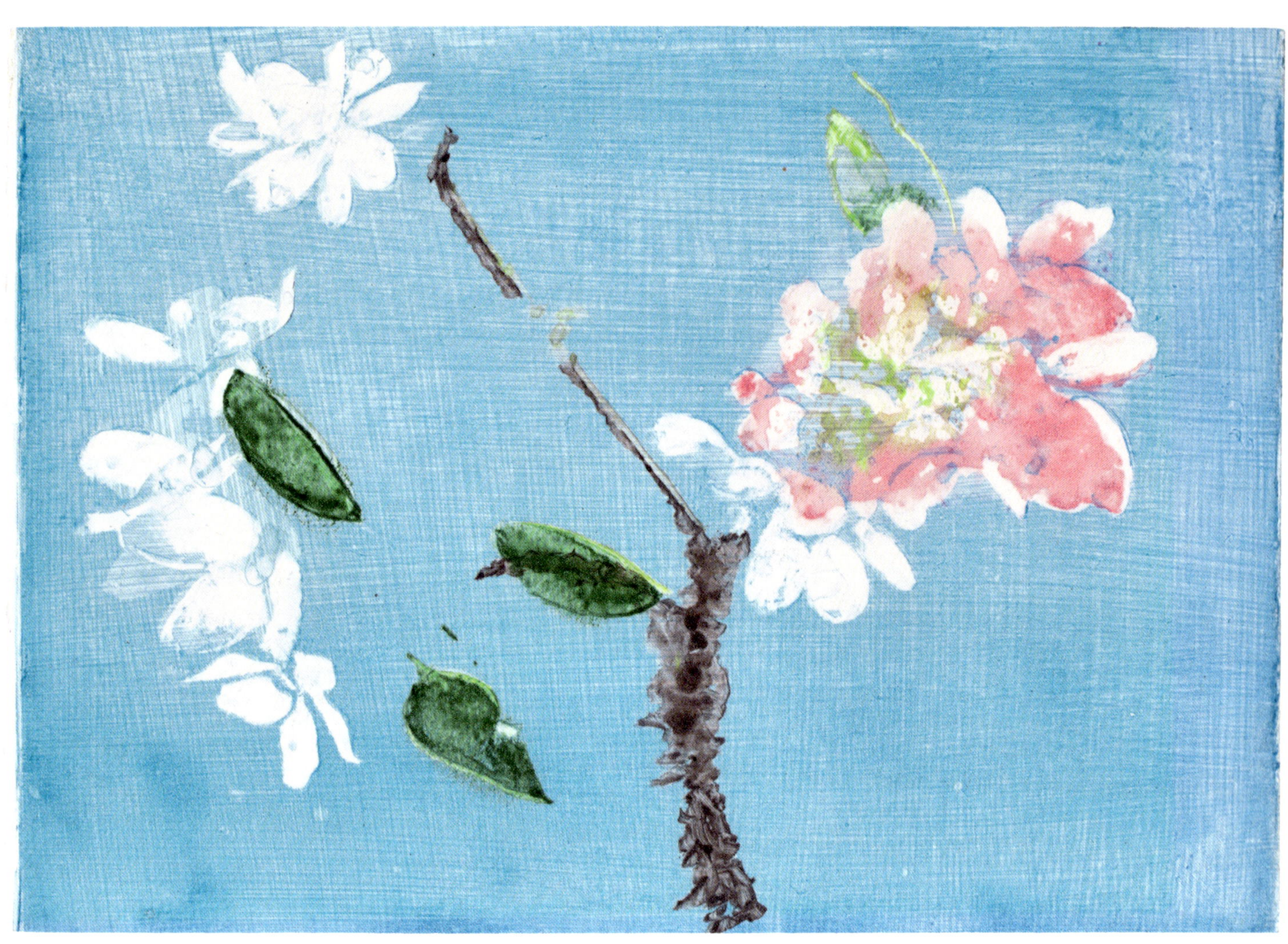

    CV51, 2020   watercolour monotype, 19.4 × 28.3 cm

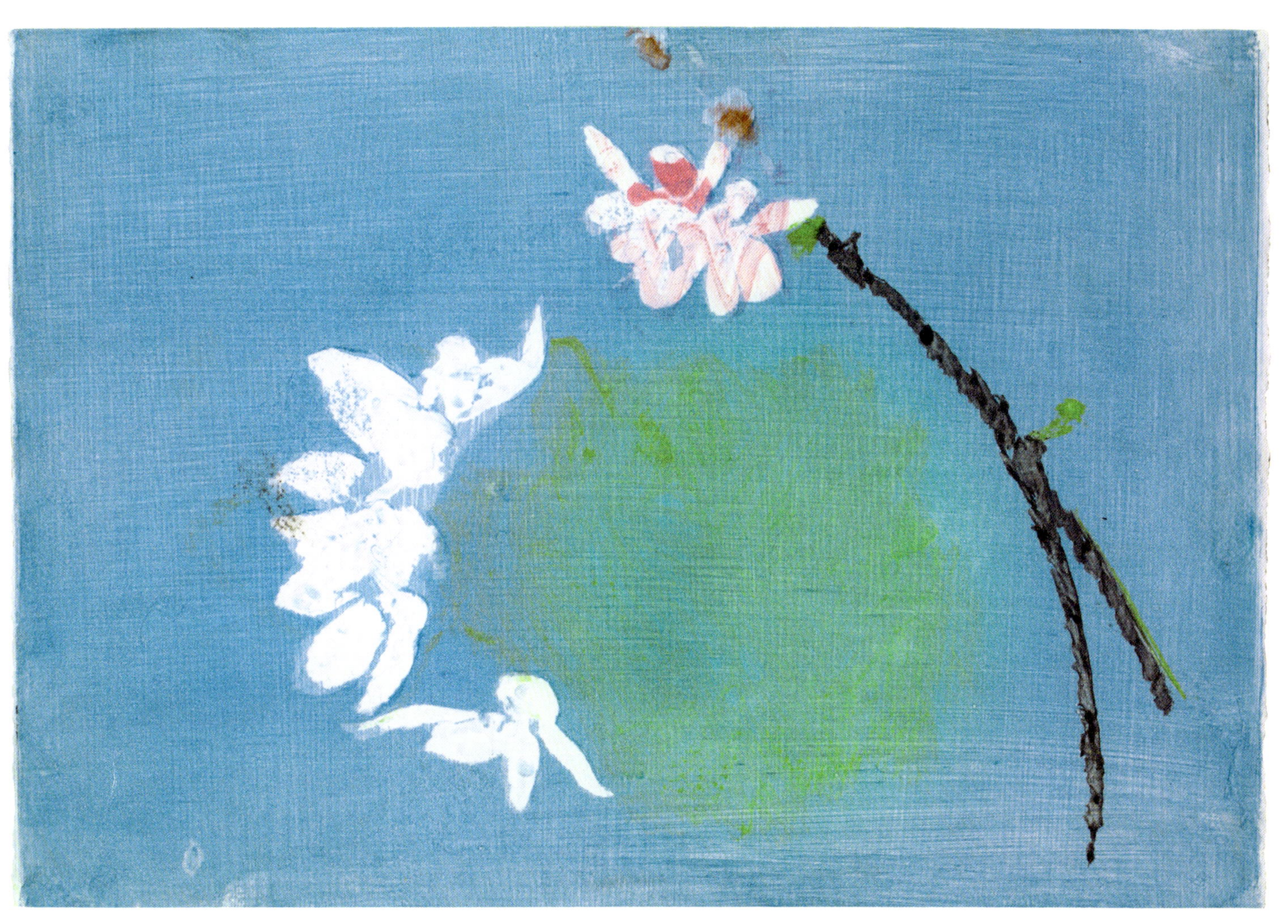

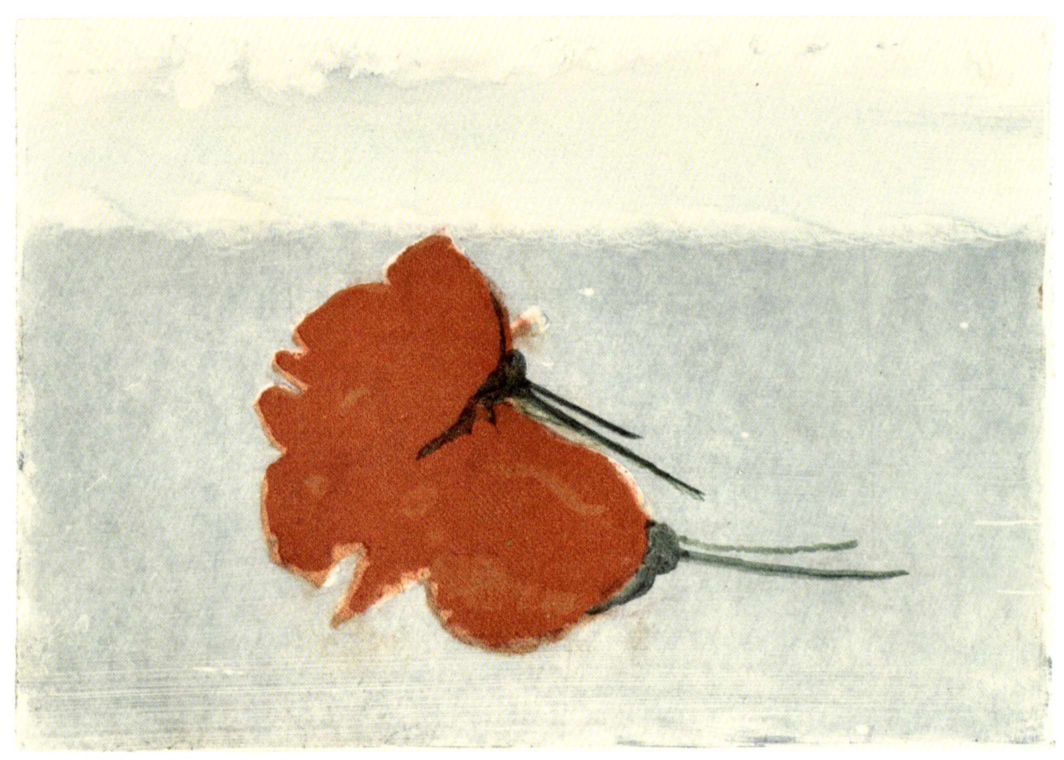

  CV53, 2020   watercolour monotype, 13.9 × 20.3 cm

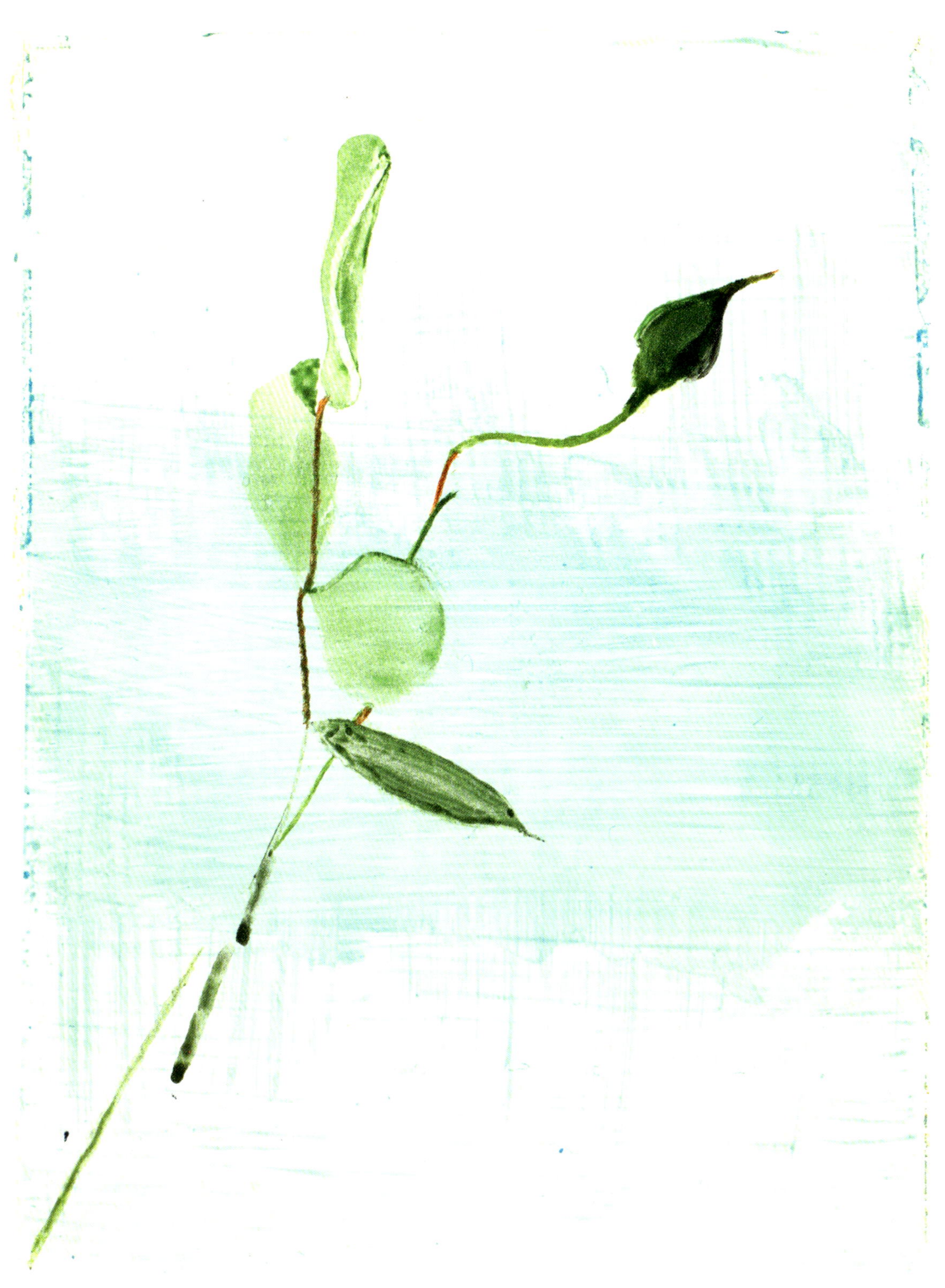

     CV56, 2020   watercolour monotype, 28 × 50.4 cm

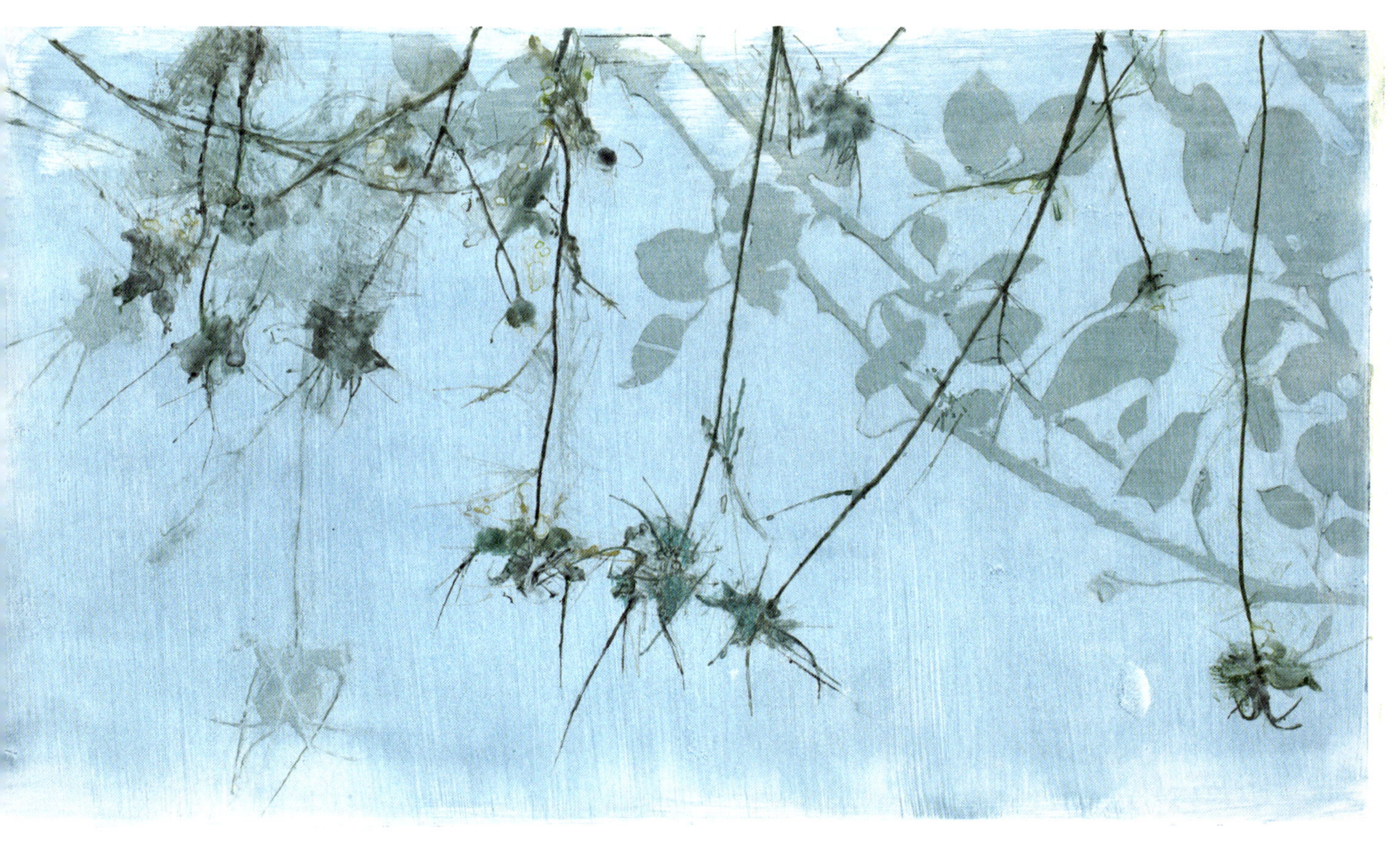

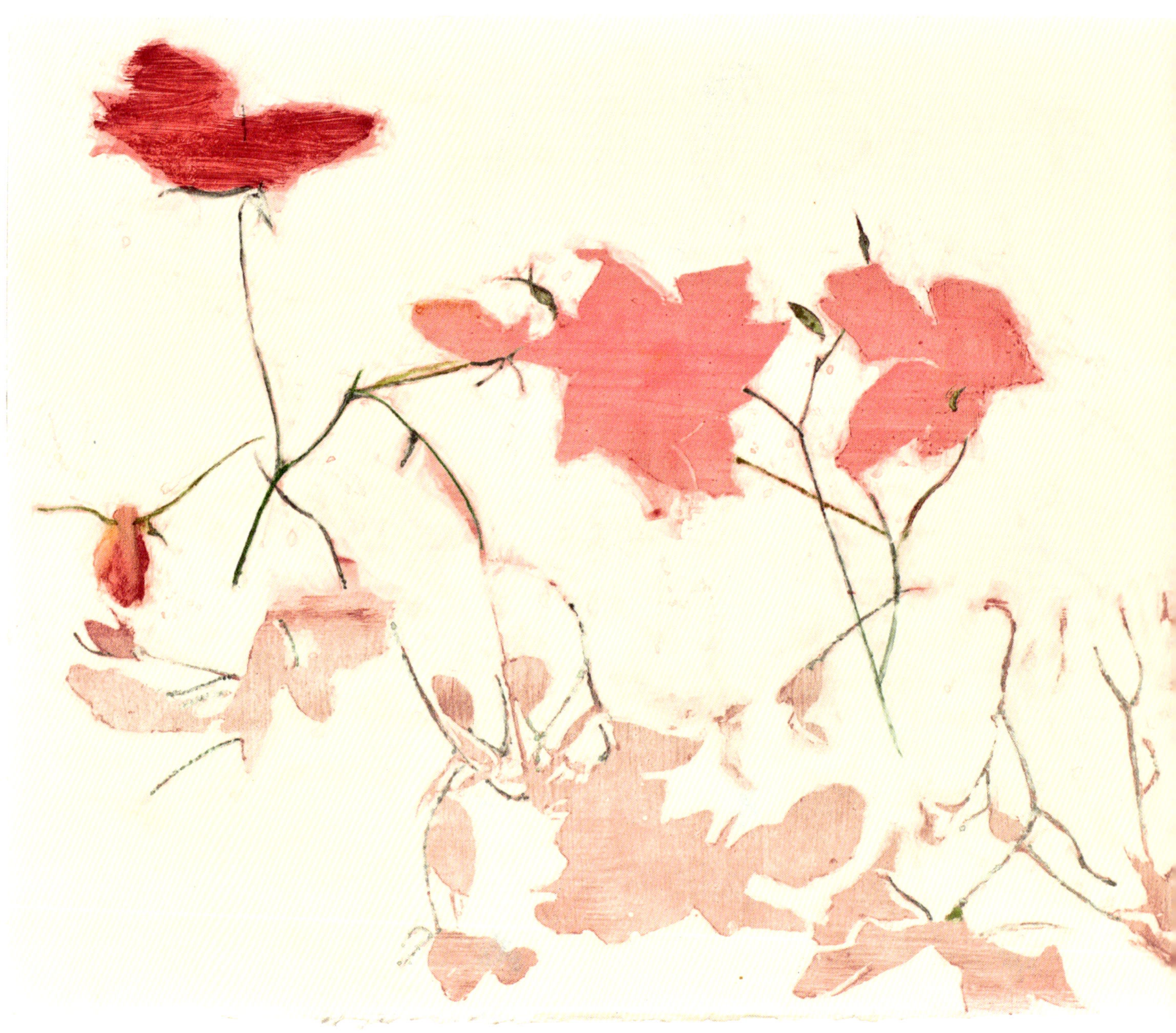

   CV57, 2020   watercolour monotype, 33.3 × 40.2 cm

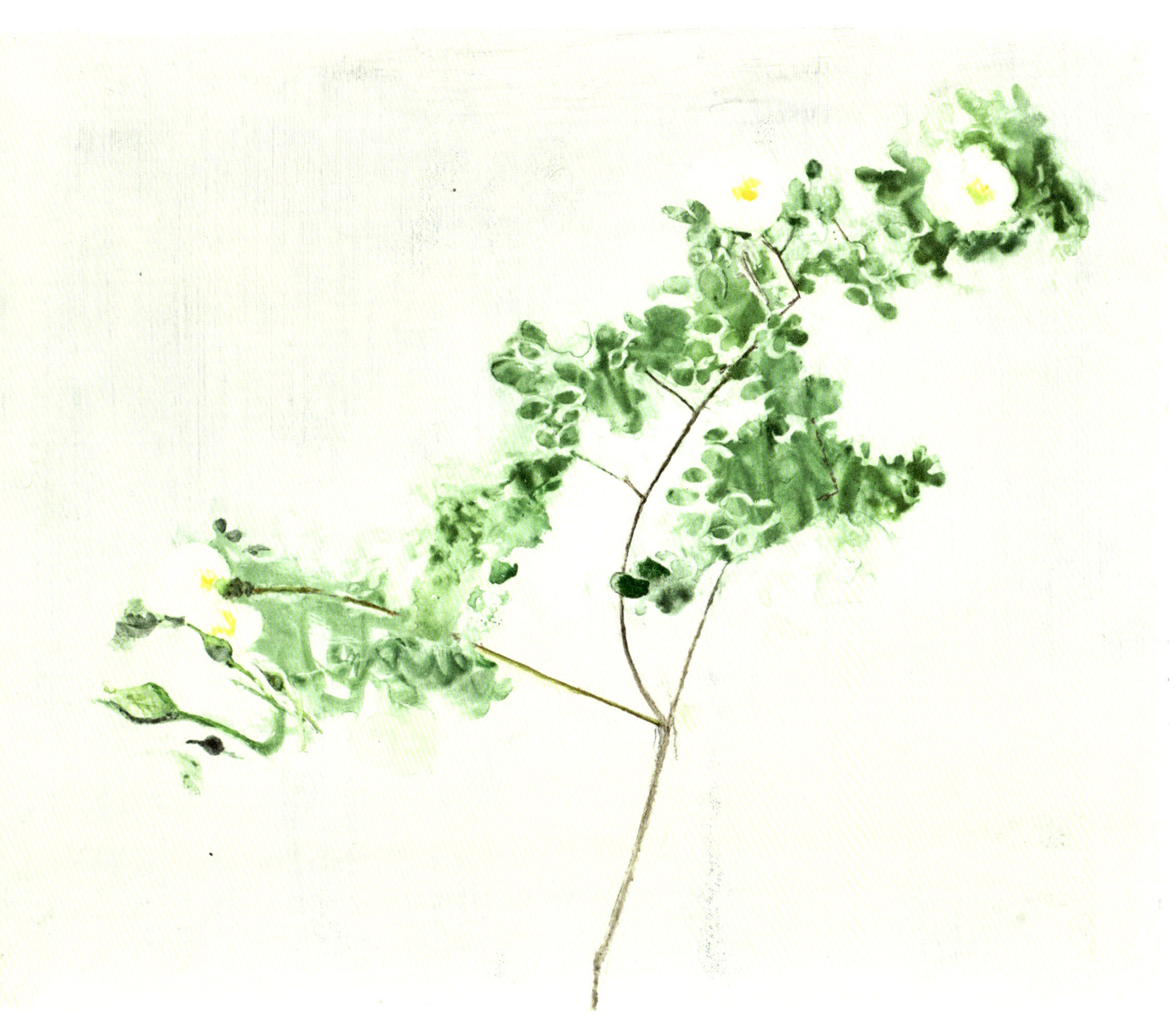

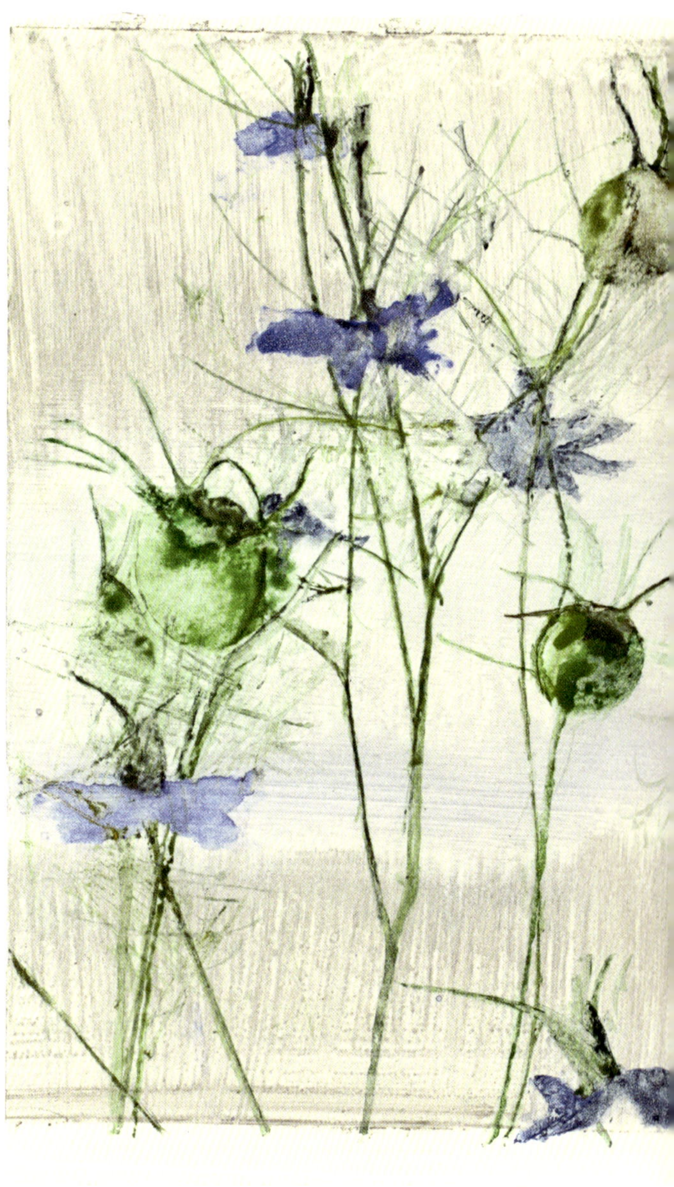

84   *CV59*, 2020   watercolour monotype, 21.2 × 42.7 cm

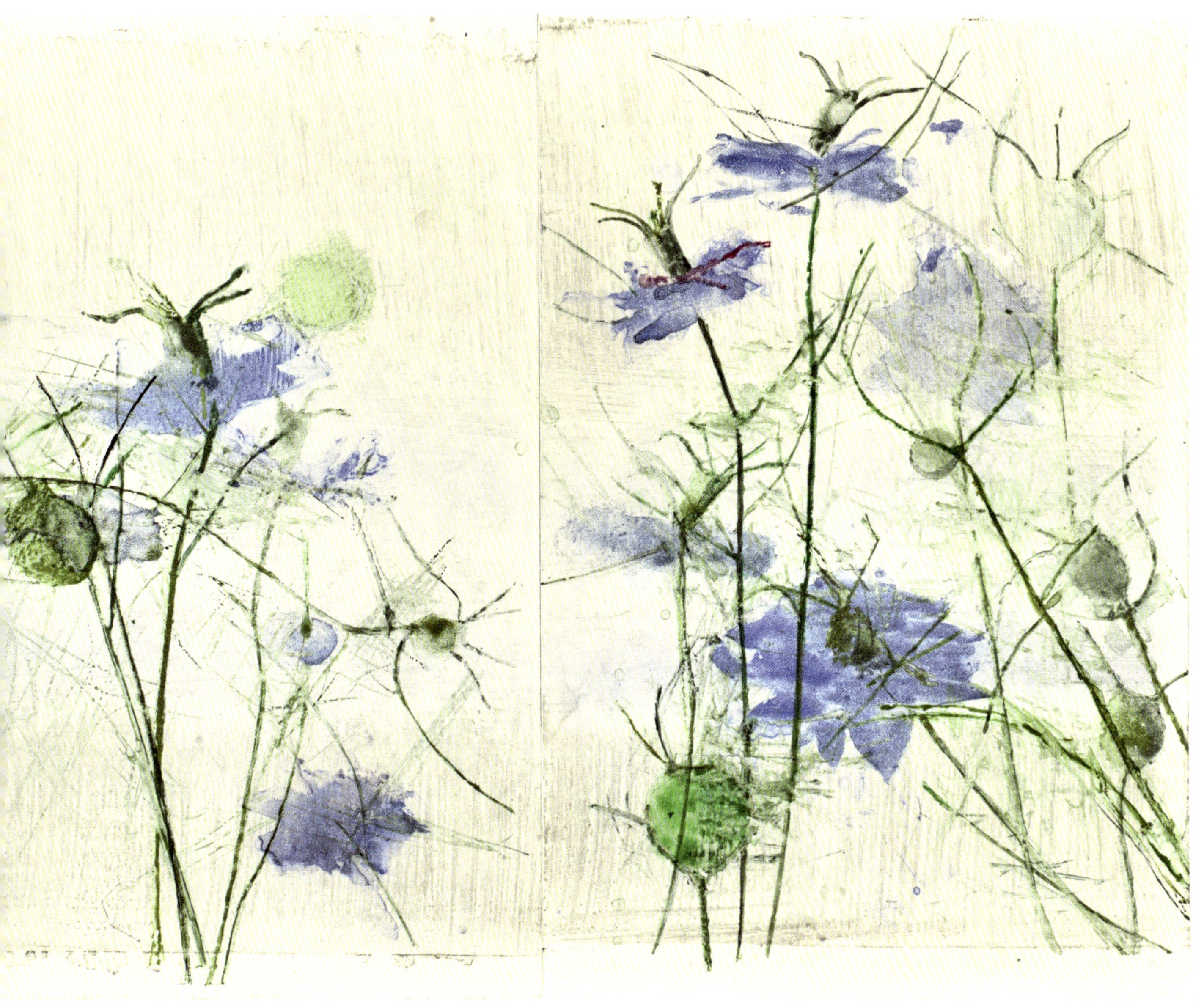

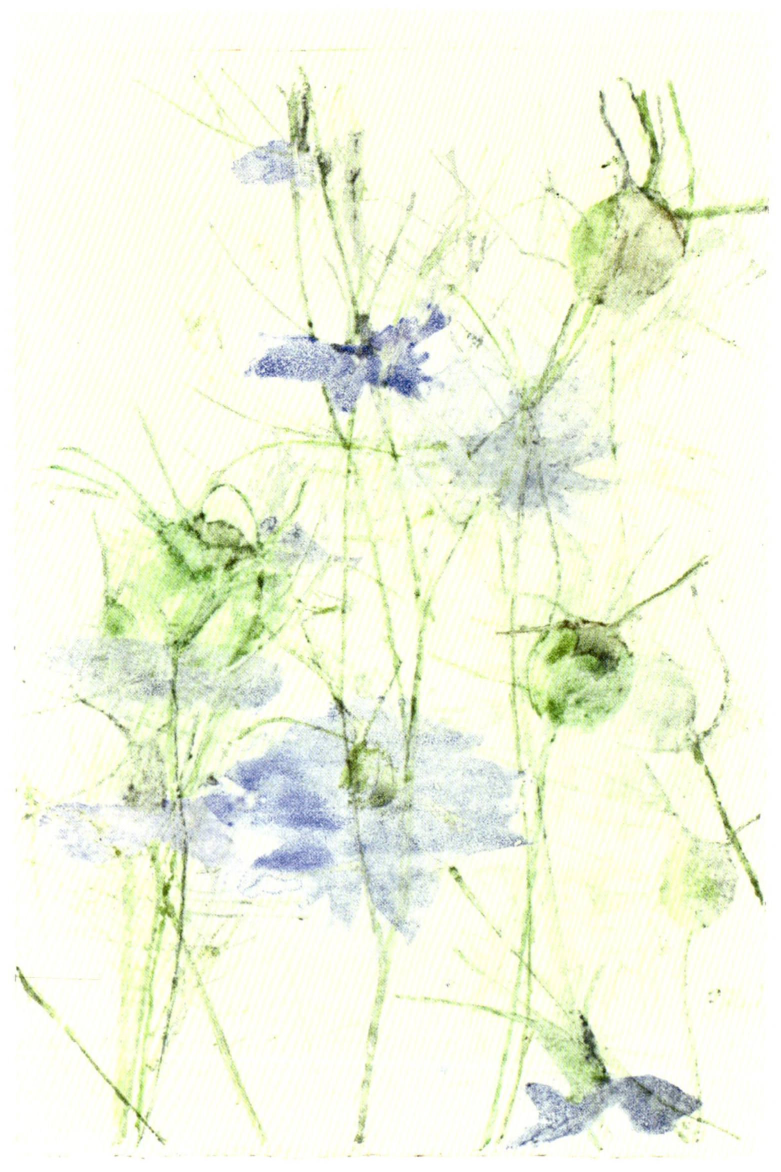

86   *CV60*, 2020   watercolour monotype, 21.3 × 14.4 cm

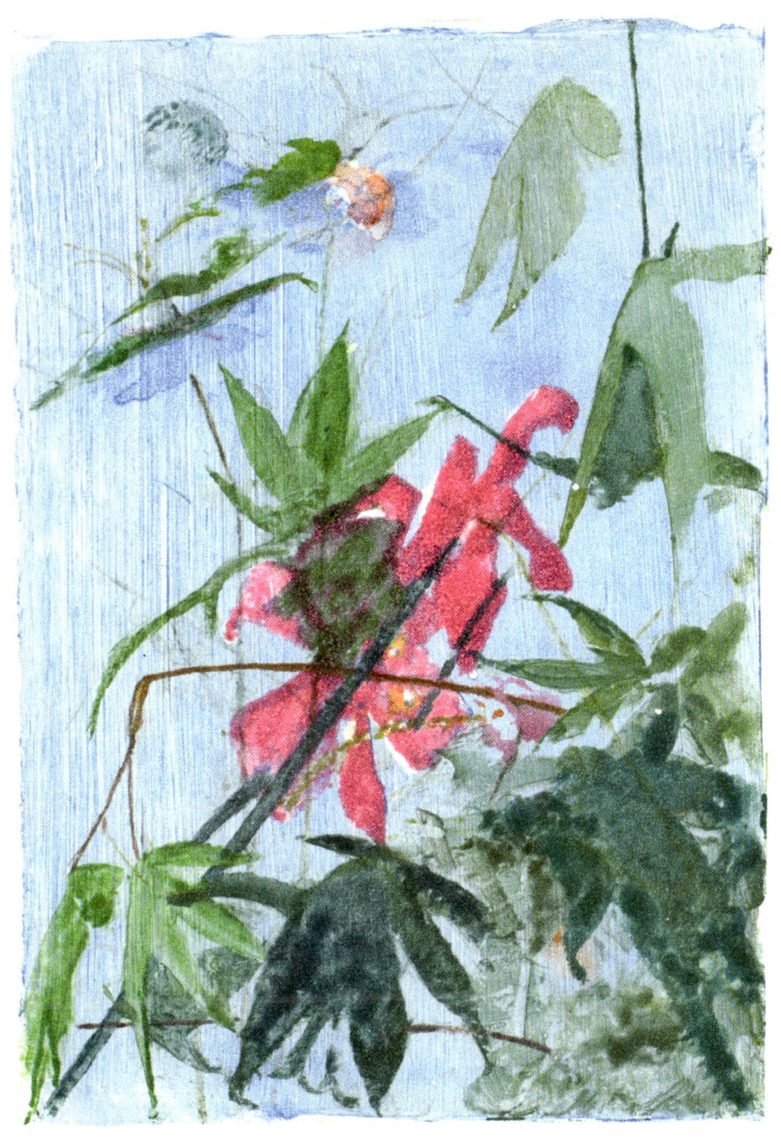

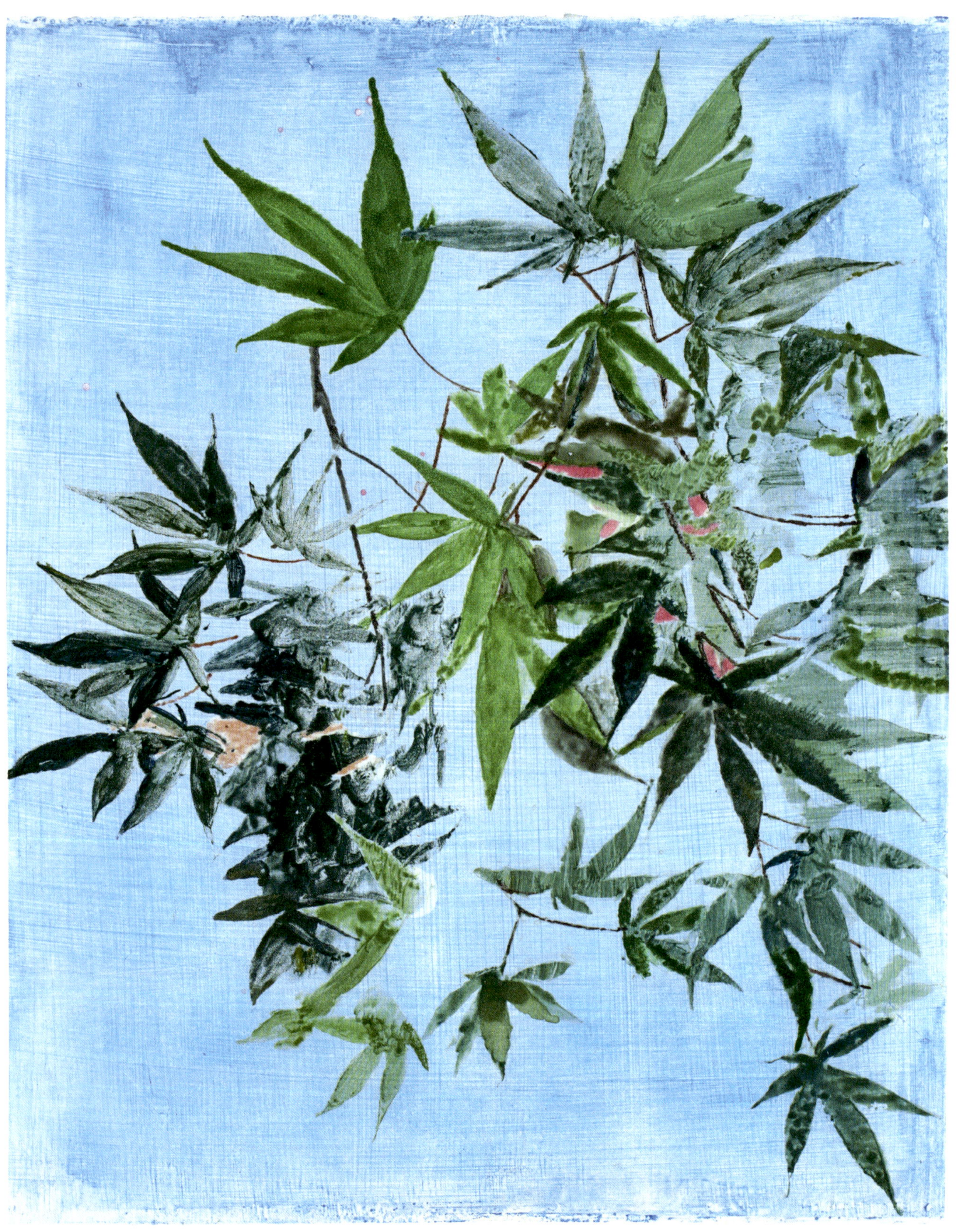

  CV62, 2020   watercolour monotype, 40.8 × 32.8 cm

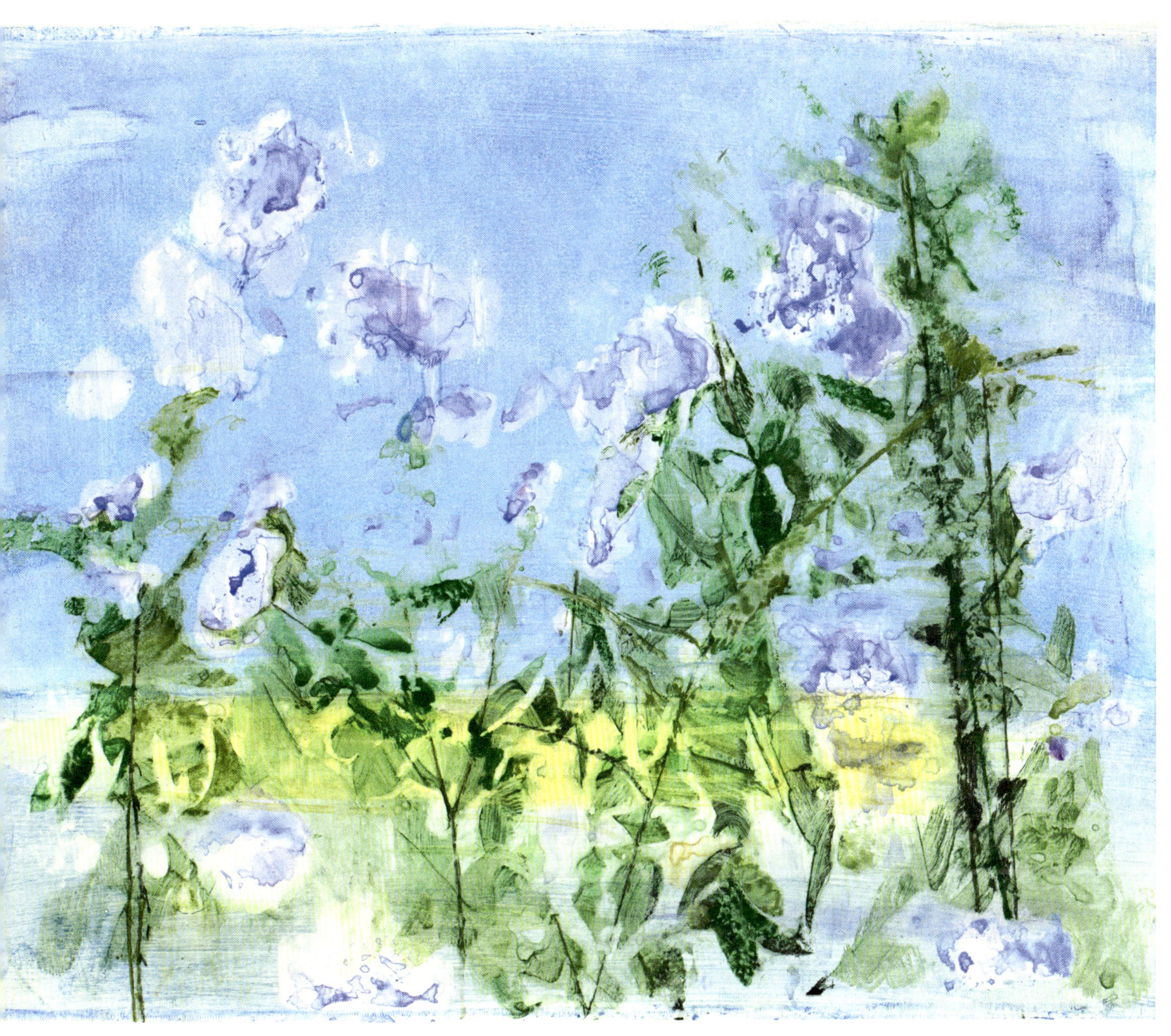

CV63, 2020   watercolour monotype, 33.2 × 40.2 cm   89

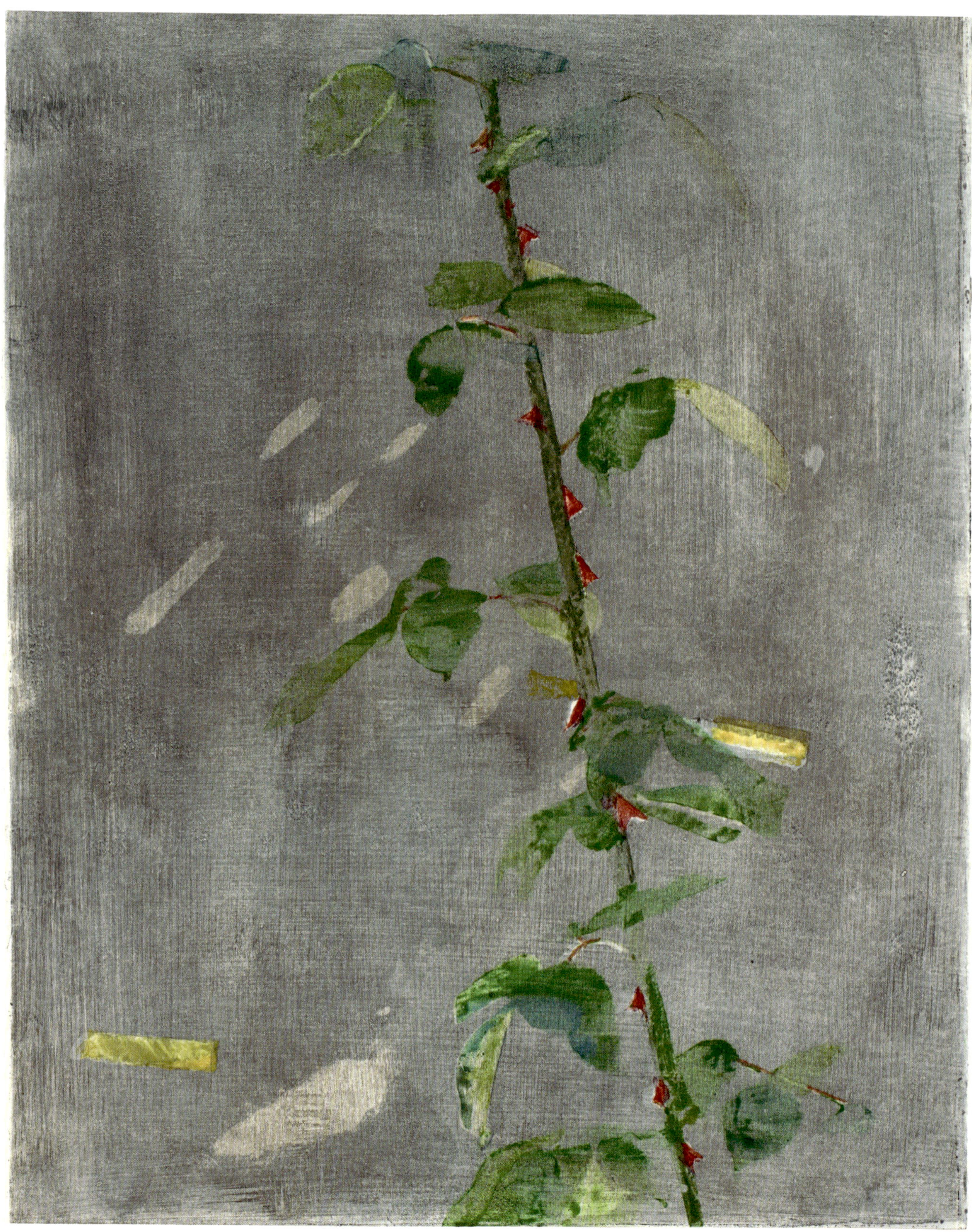

  CV64, 2020   watercolour monotype, 40.3 × 33.2 cm

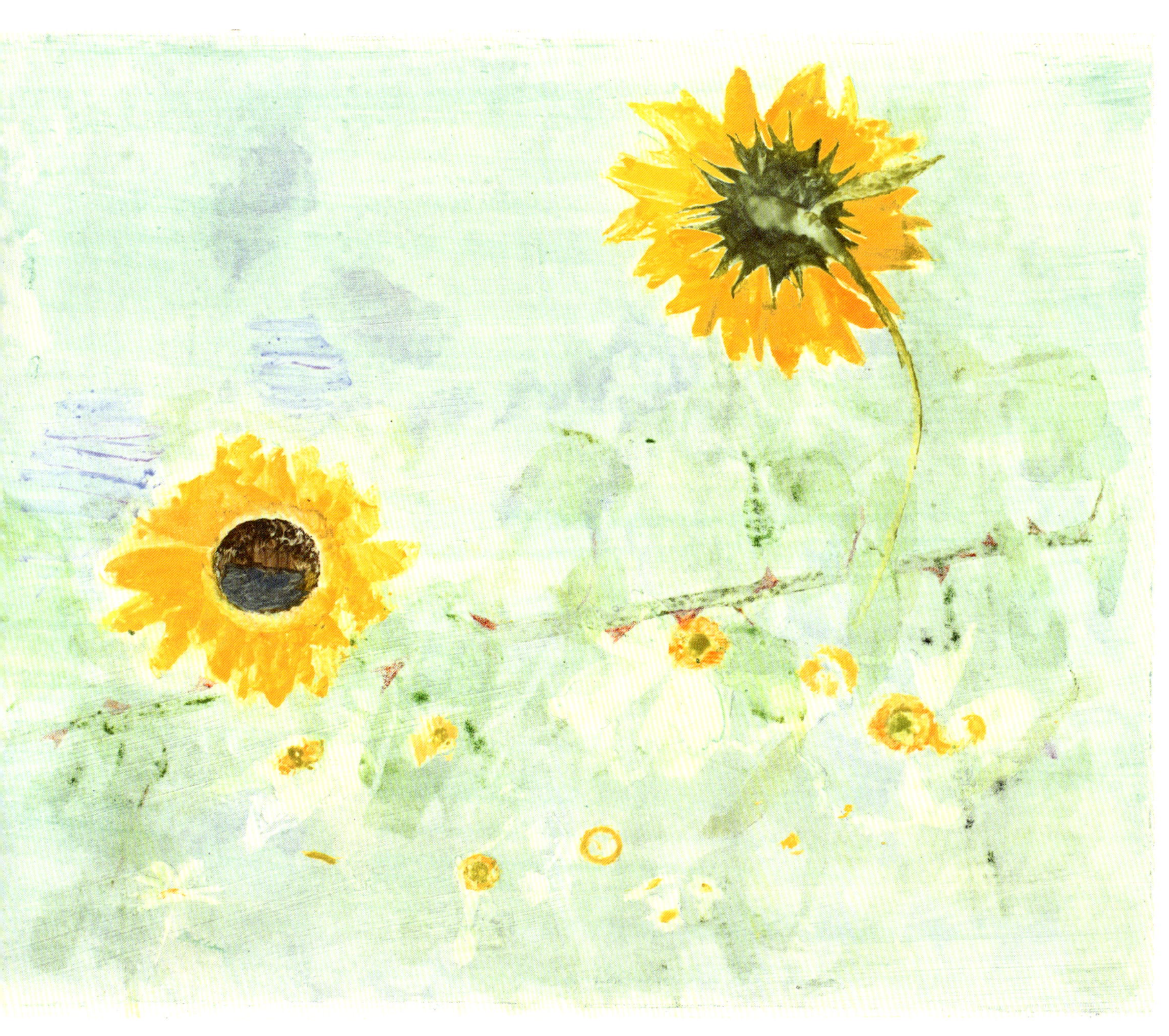

    CV65, 2020   watercolour monotype, 27.6 × 50.3 cm

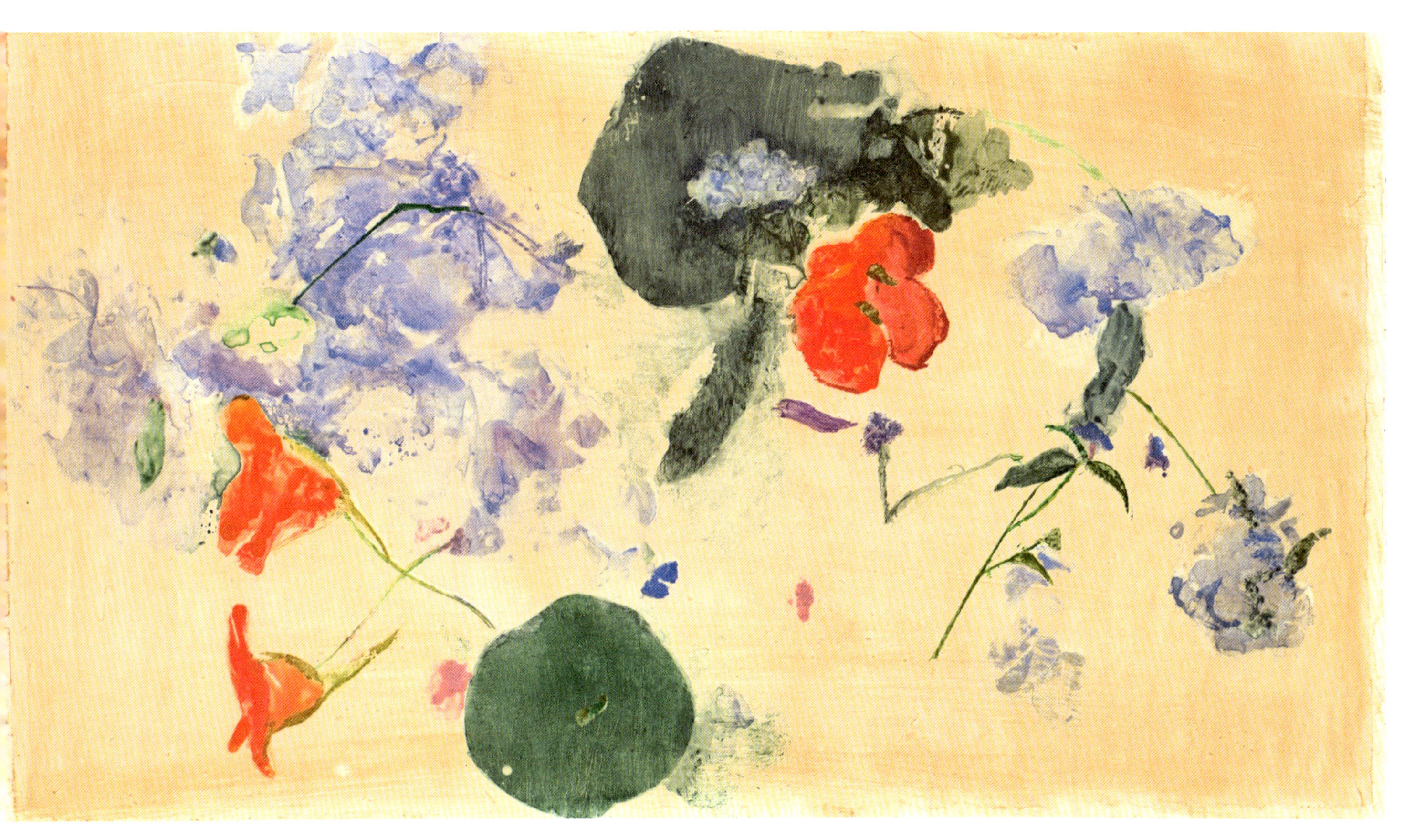

  CV66, 2020   watercolour monotype, 27.6 × 49.7 cm

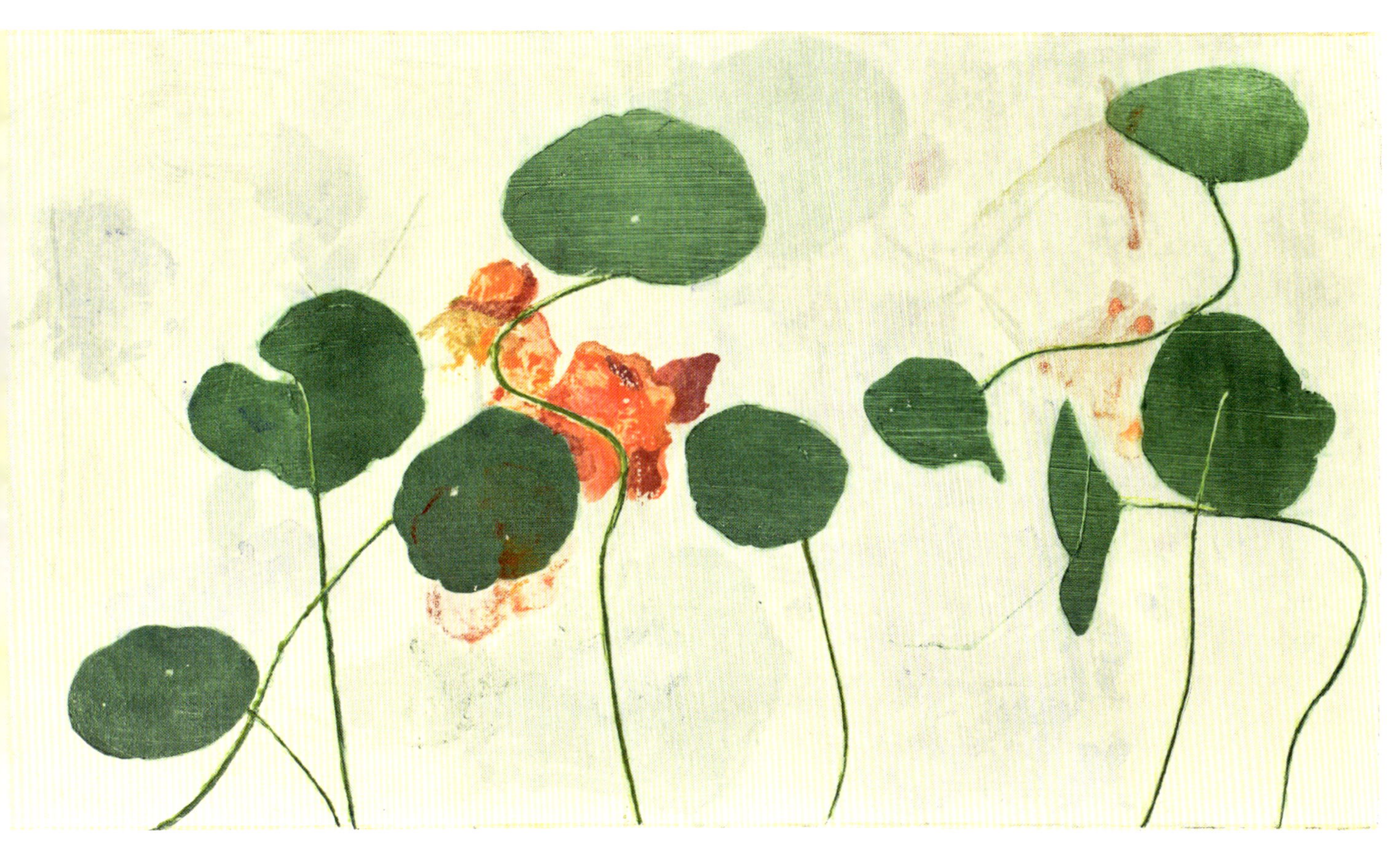

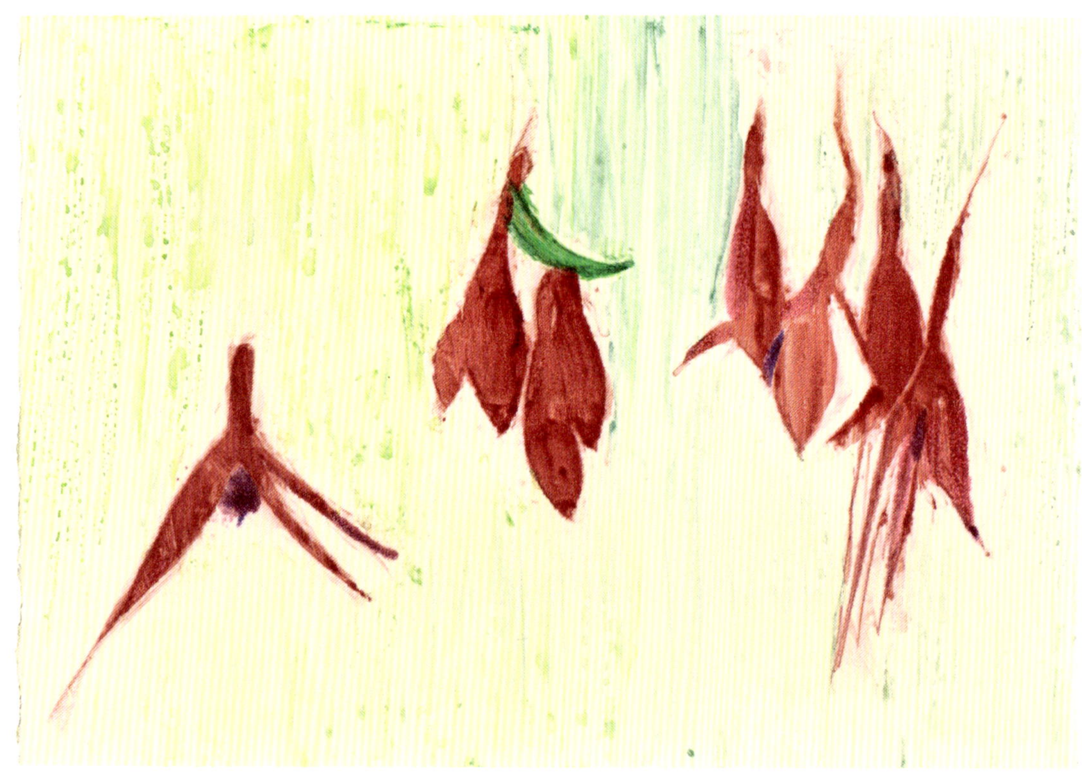

     CV72, 2020   watercolour monotype, 13.9 × 20.2 cm

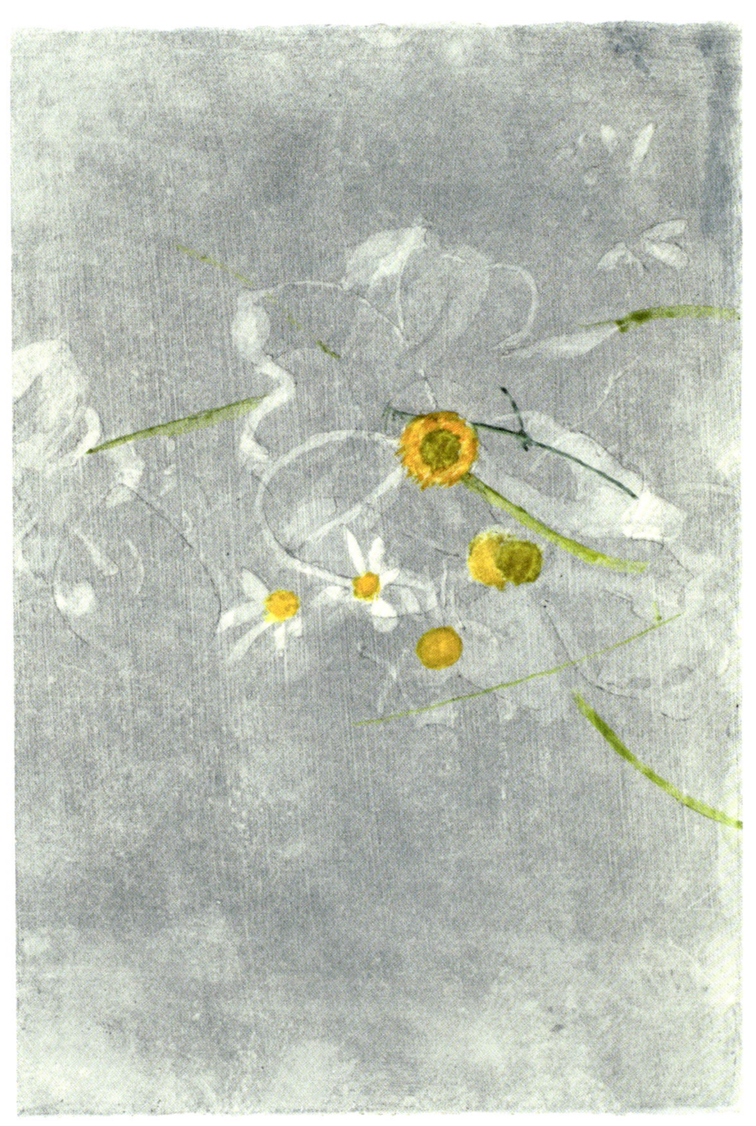

   CV73, 2020   watercolour monotype, 27.1 × 49.7 cm

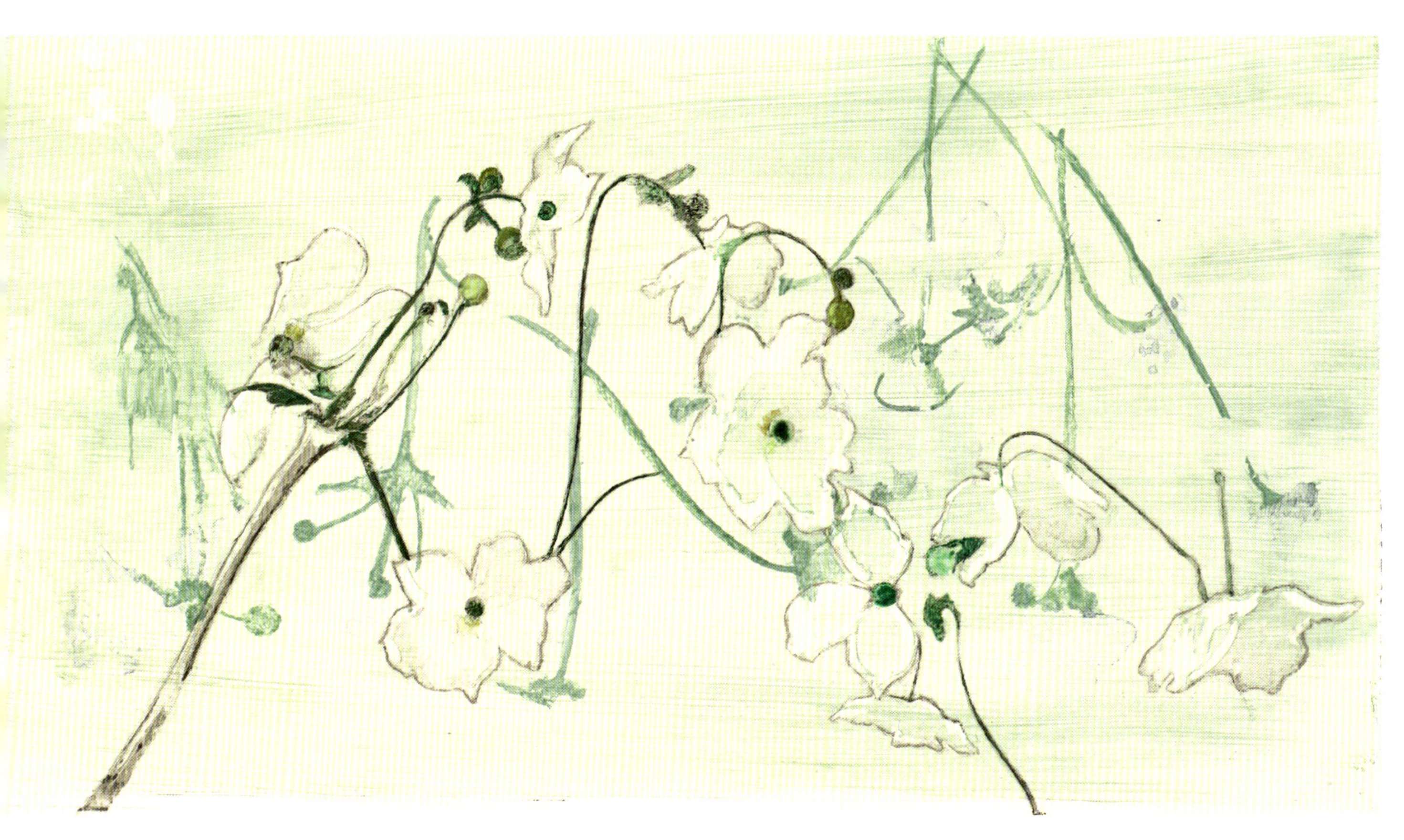

     CV75, 2020   watercolour monotype, 28.3 × 19.3 cm

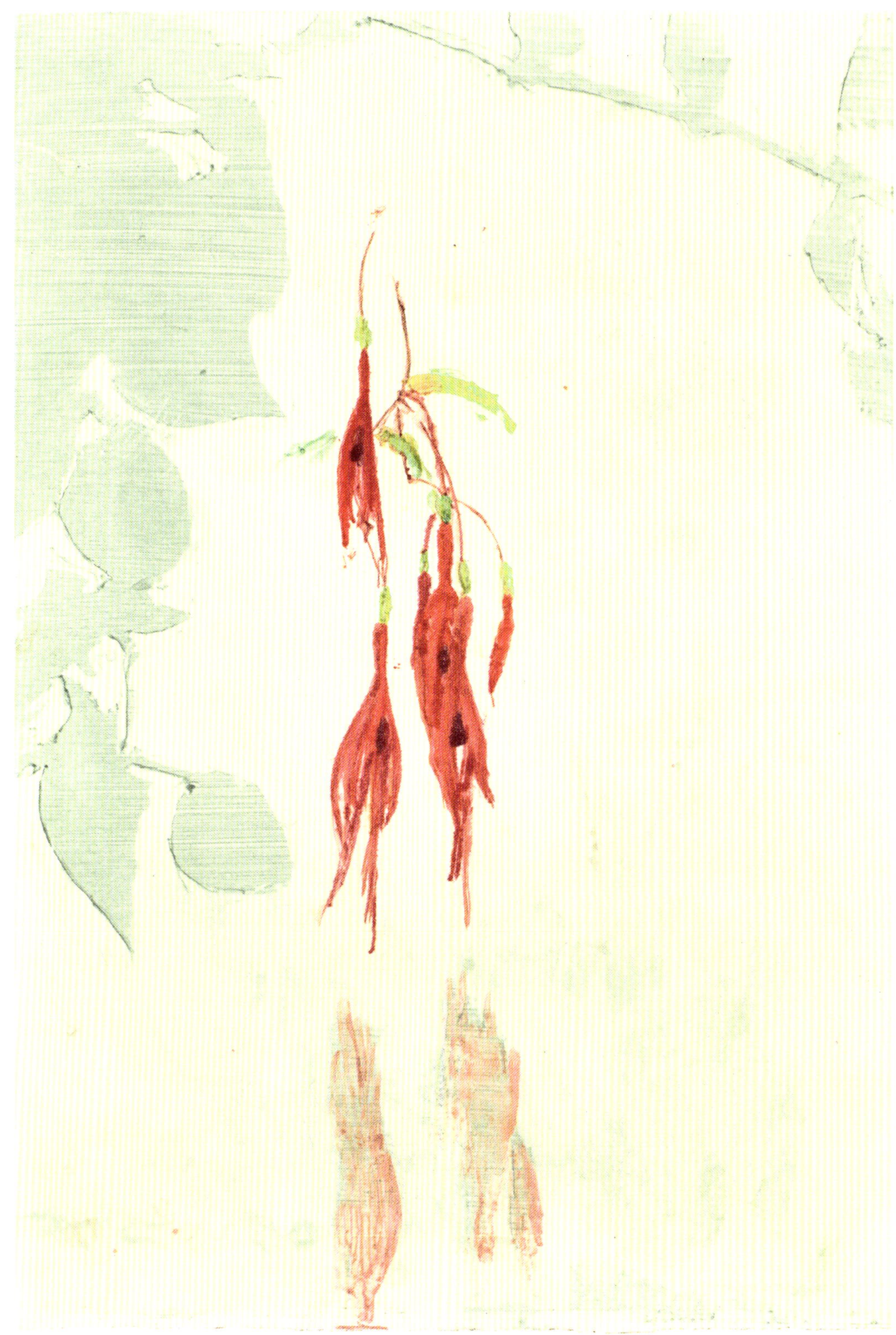

	CV77, 2020	watercolour monotype, 27.1 × 49.7 cm

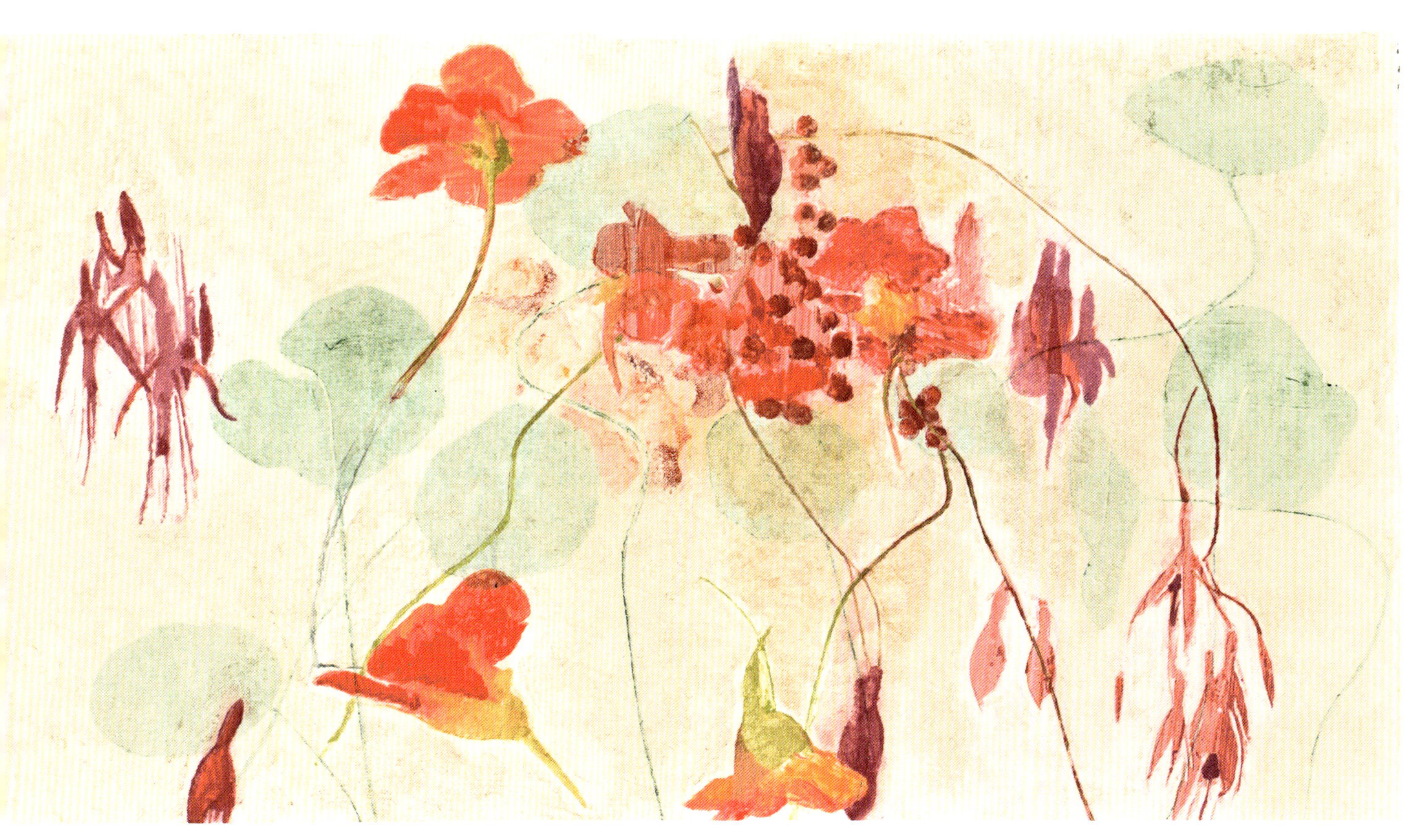

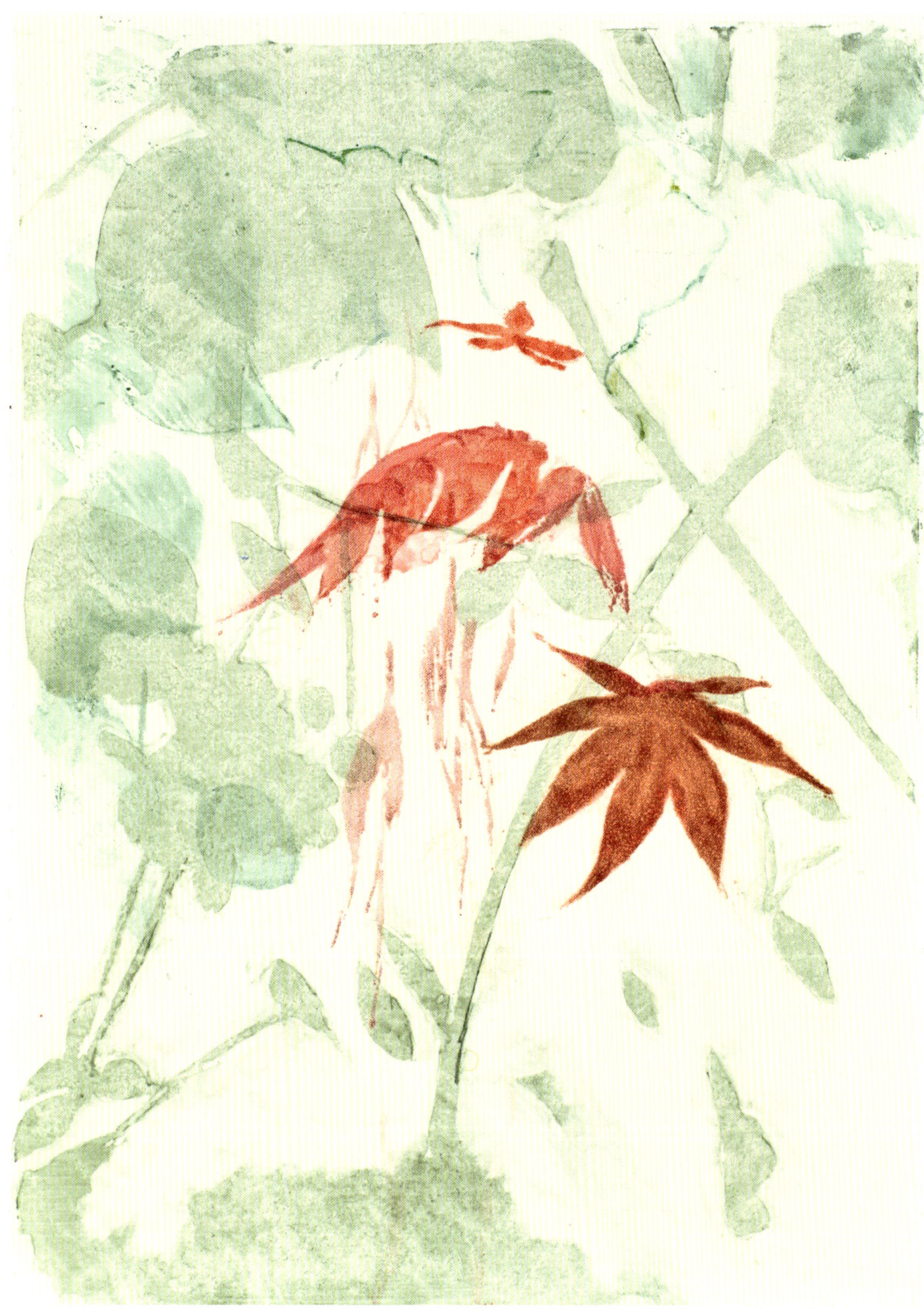

    CV78, 2020   watercolour monotype, 28.4 × 20.5 cm

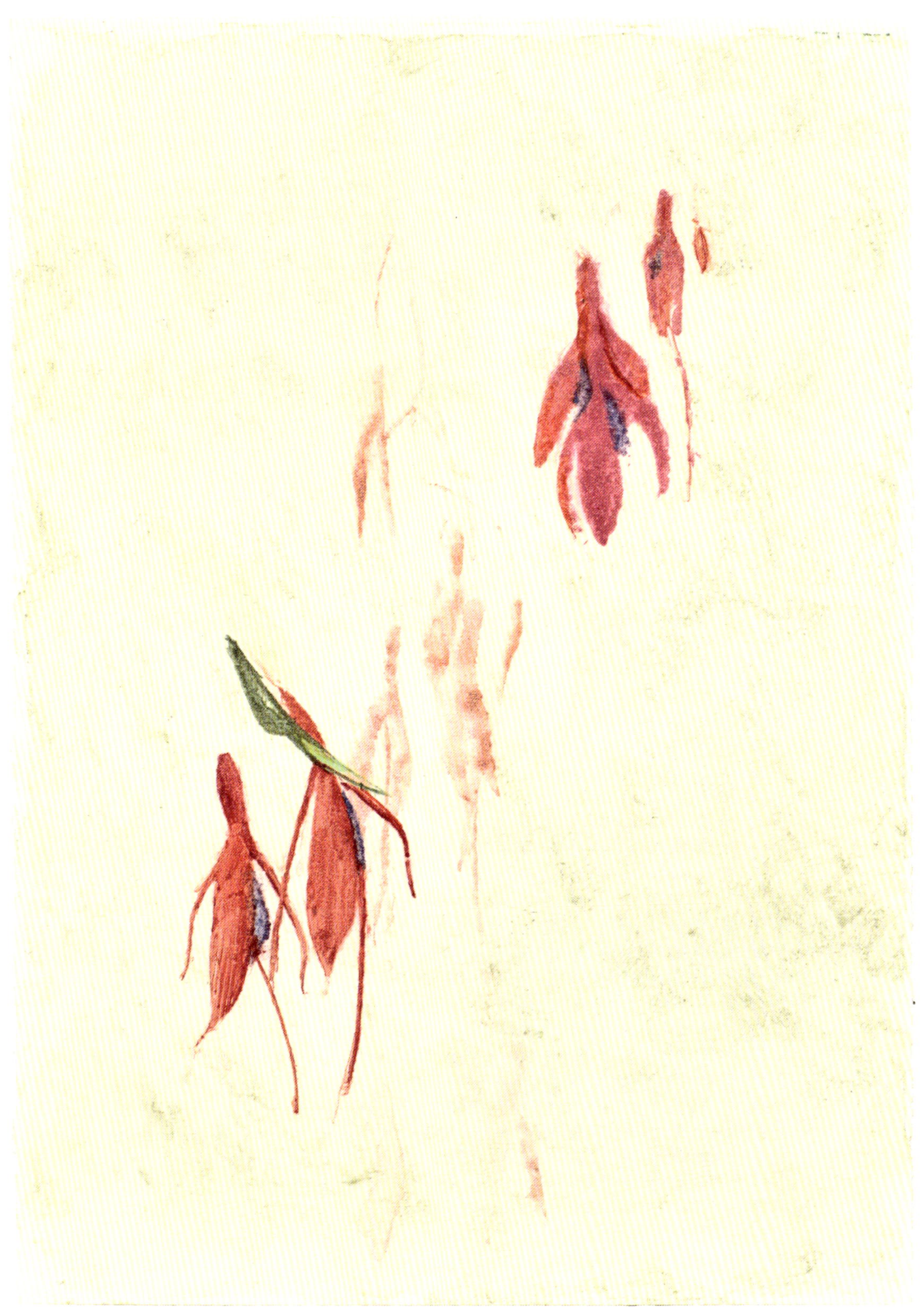

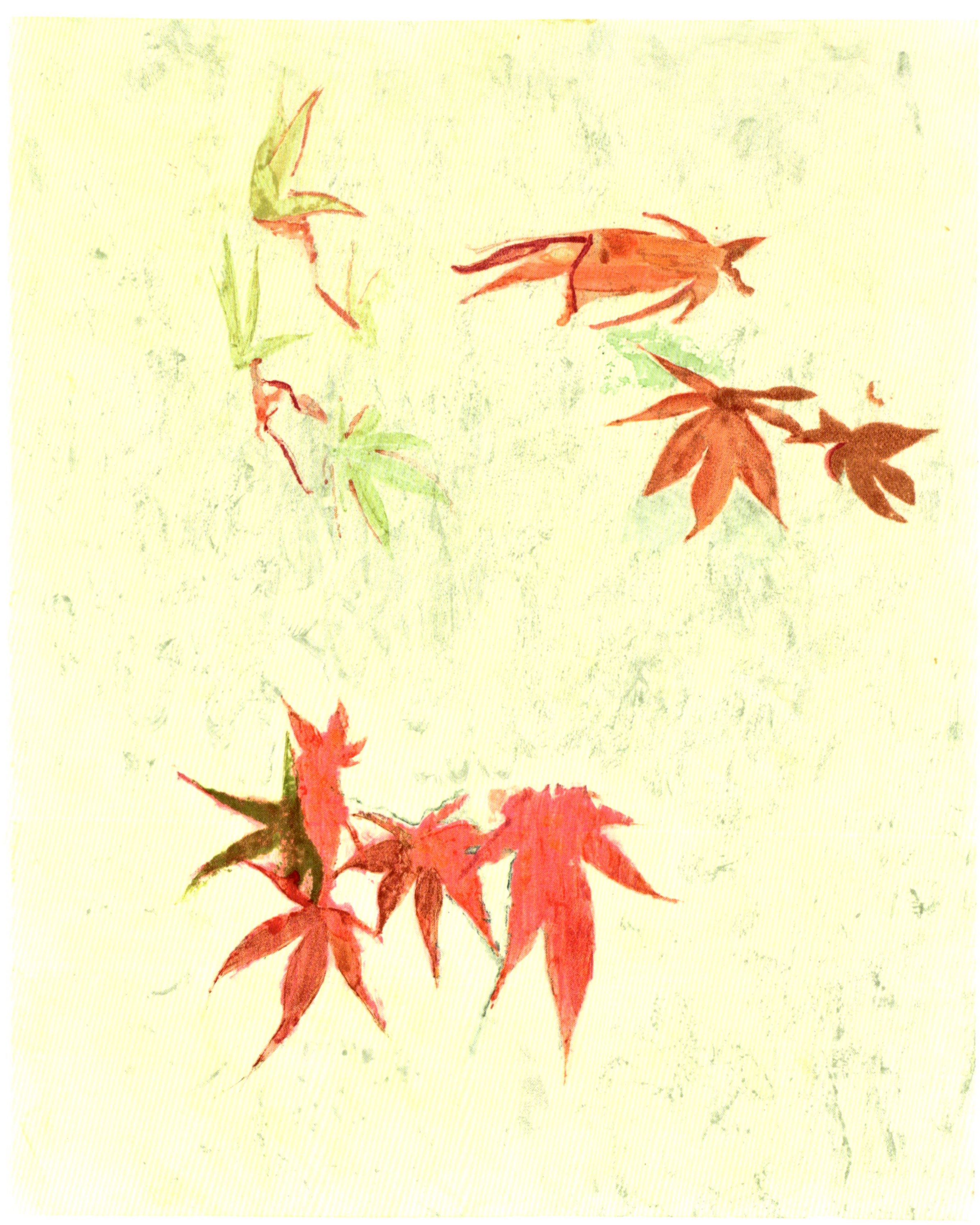

106   *CV80*, 2020   watercolour monotype, 40.2 × 33.2 cm

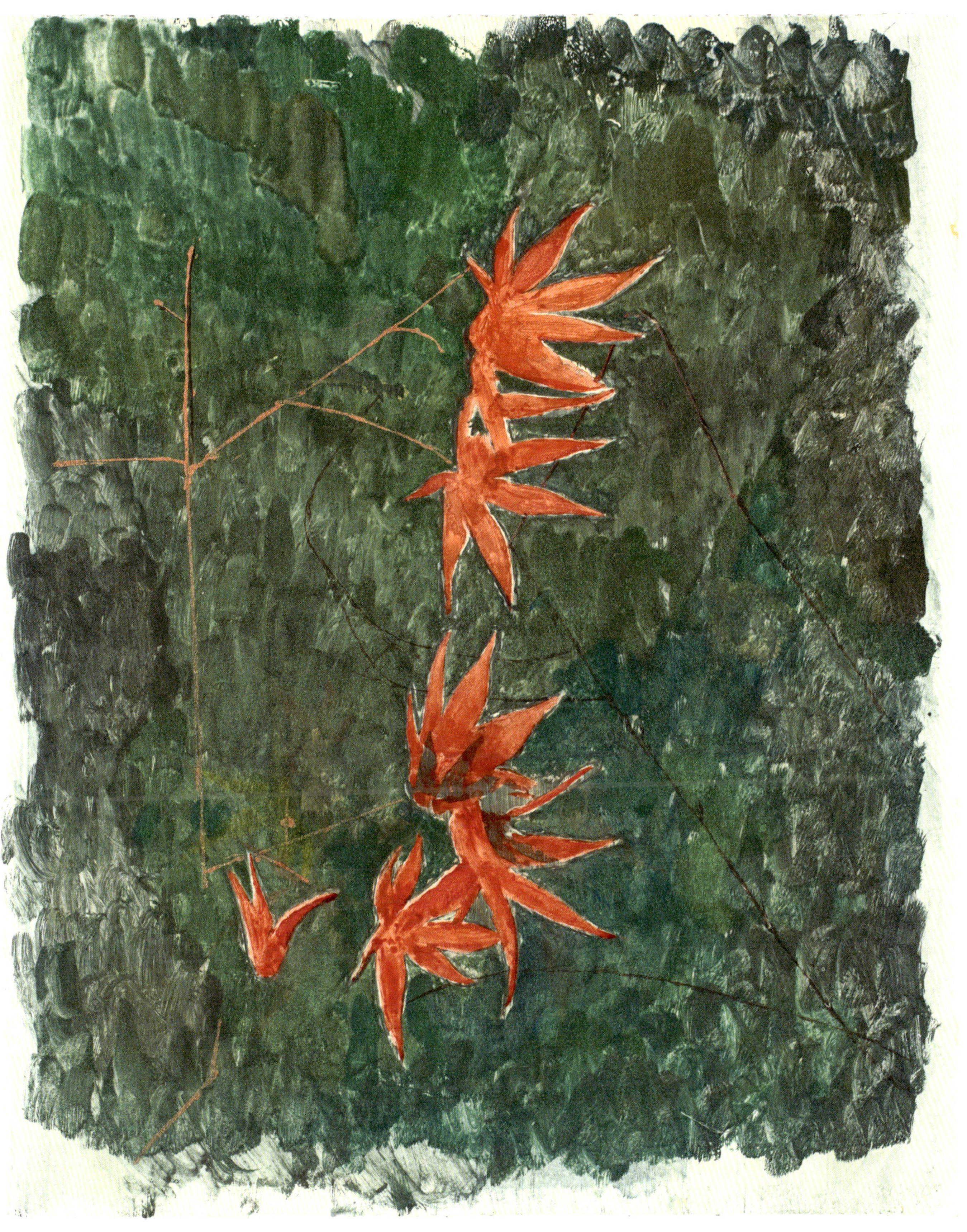

    CV83, 2020   watercolour monotype, 28.6 × 50.1 cm

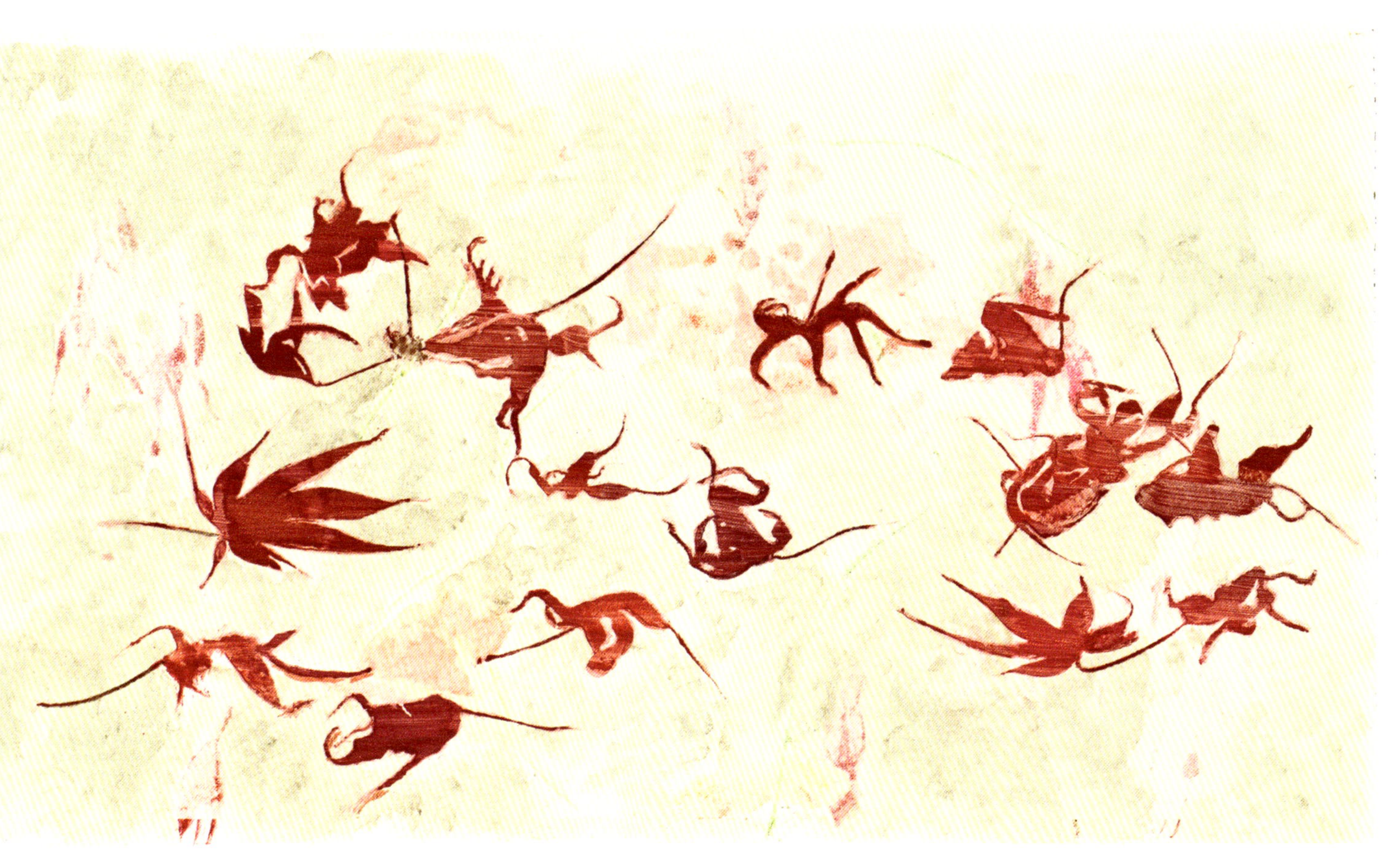

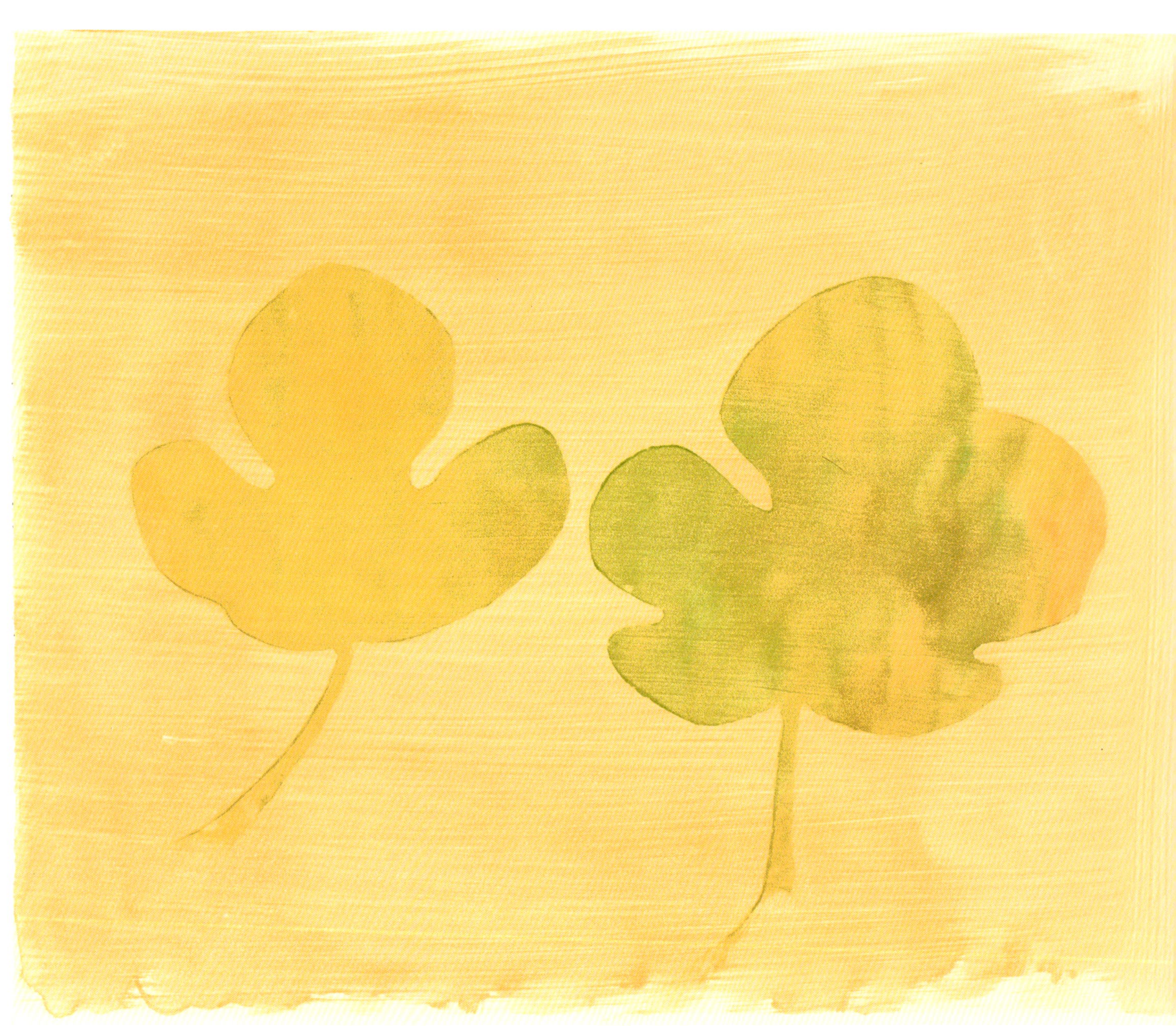

    CV84, 2020   watercolour monotype, 33.1 × 40.4 cm

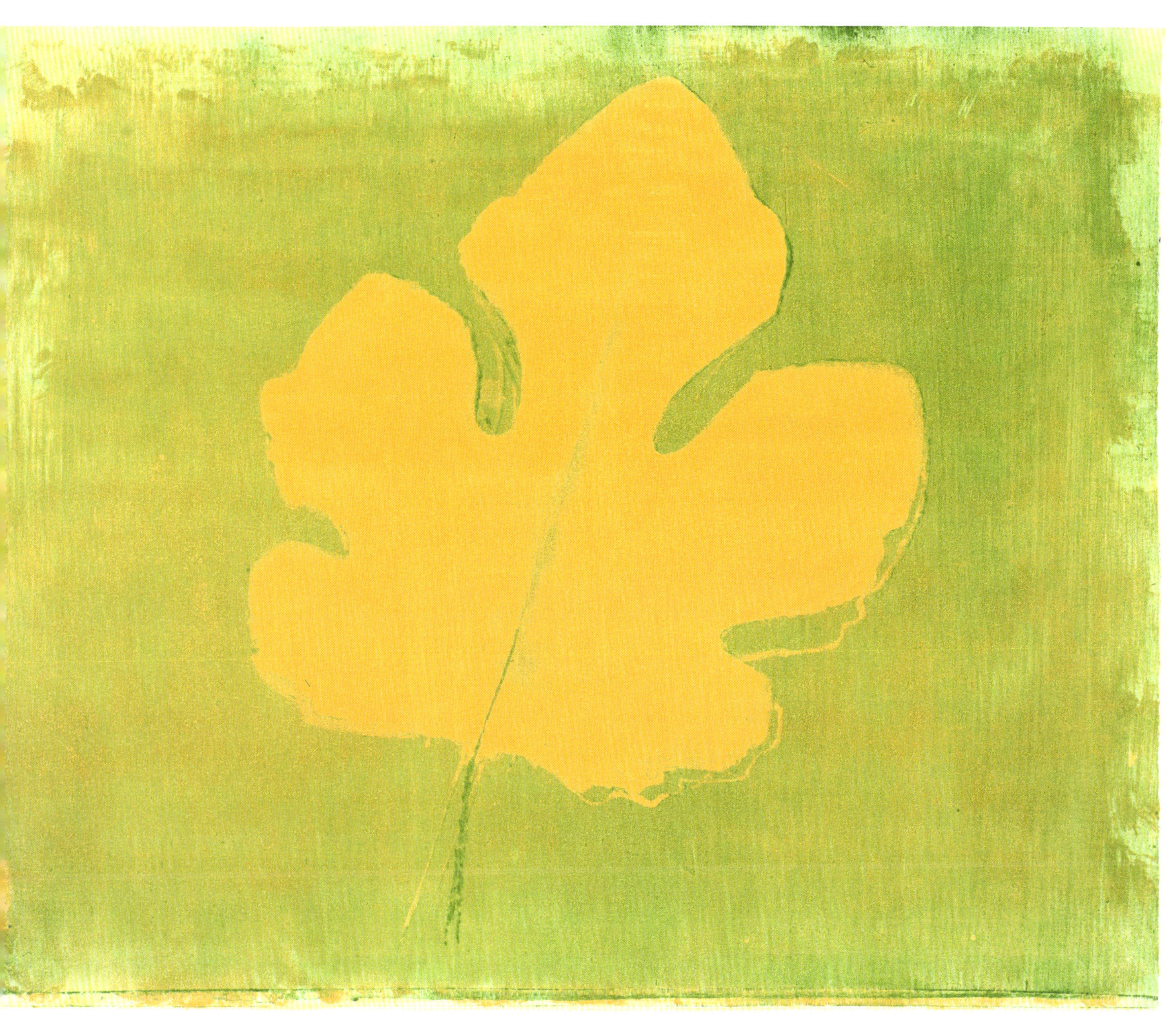

CV86, 2020   watercolour monotype, 33.2 × 40.4 cm   111

    CV87, 2020   watercolour monotype, 20.5 × 28.7 cm

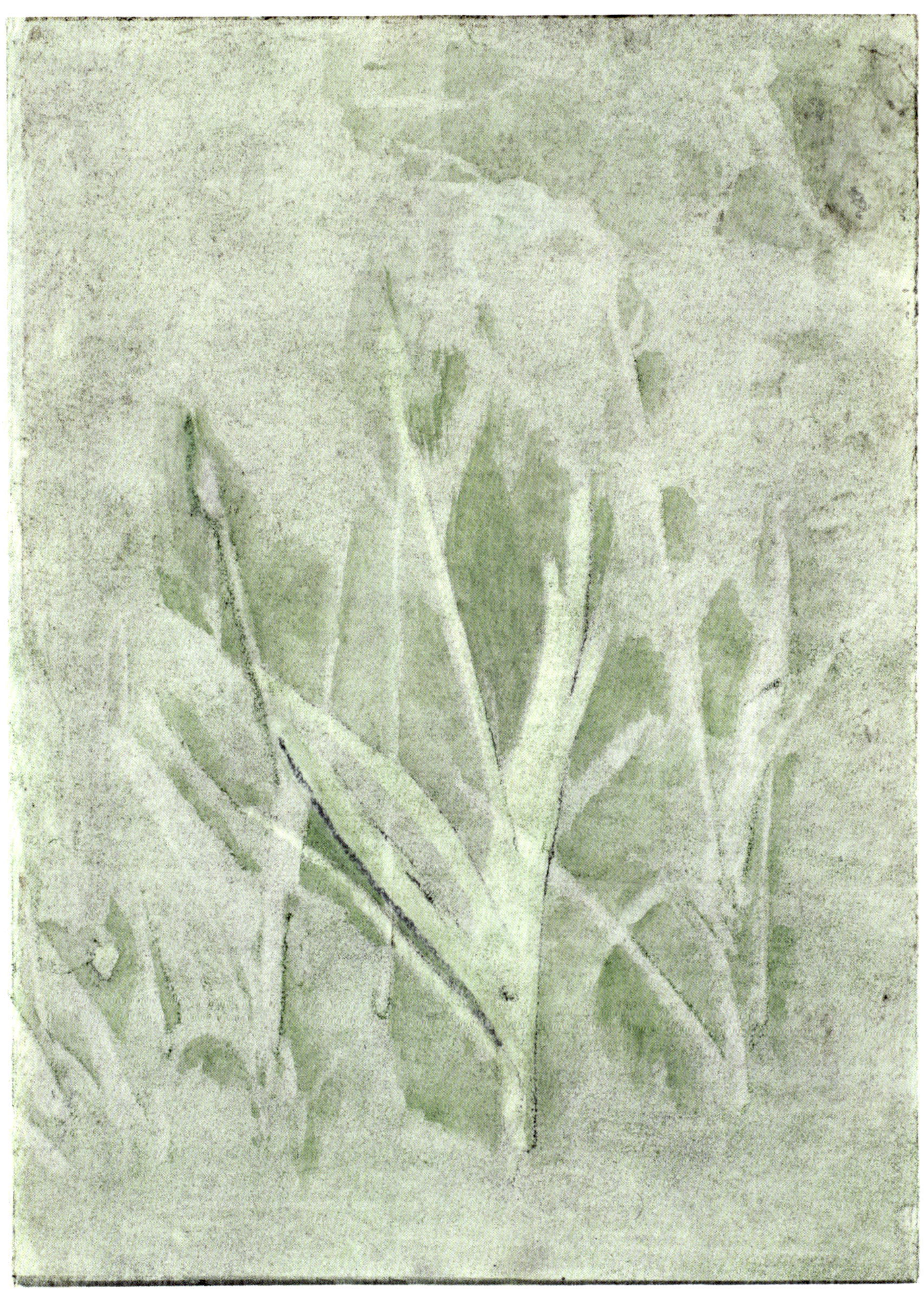

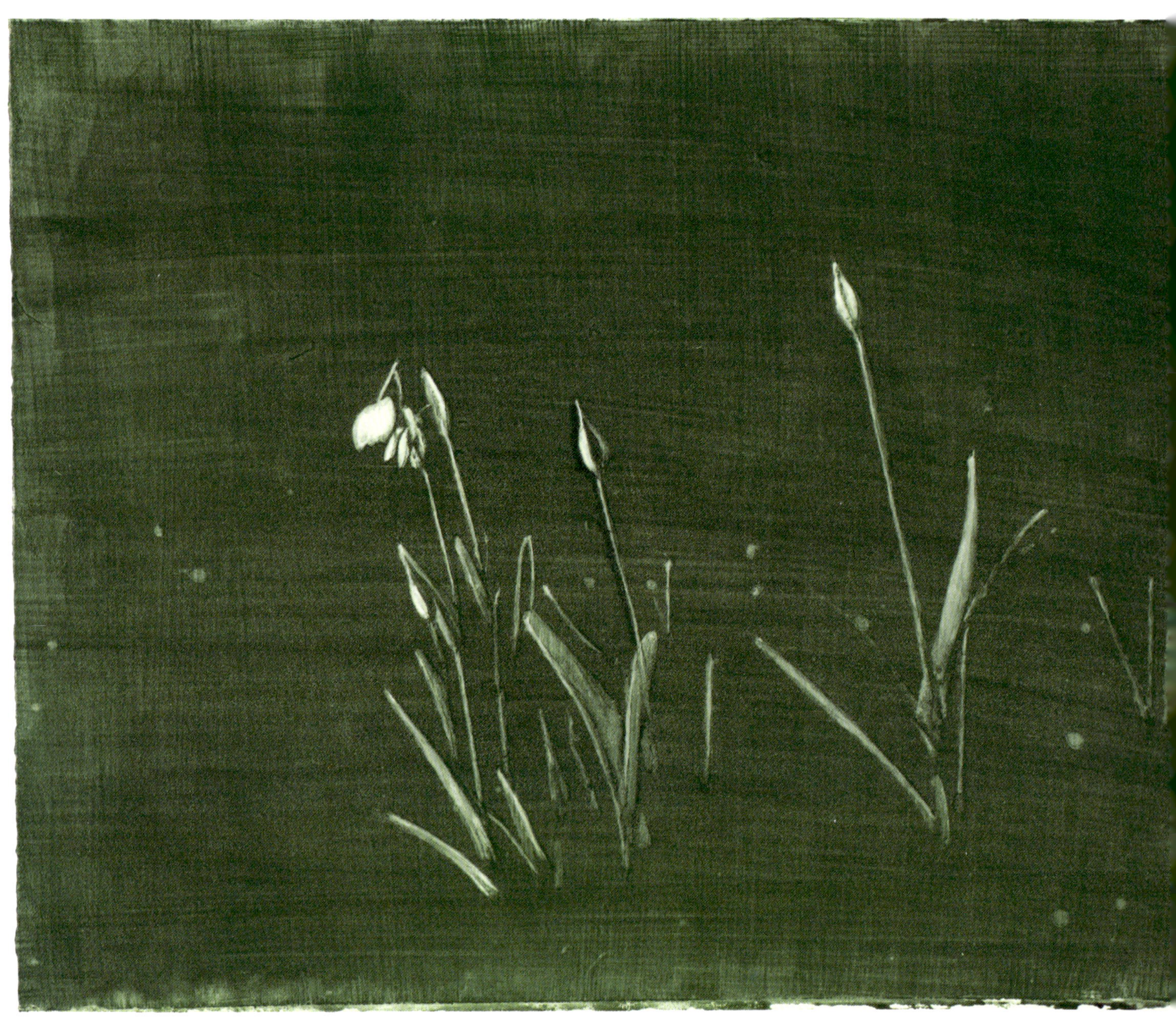

   CV95, 2021   watercolour monotype, 33.2 × 40.4 cm

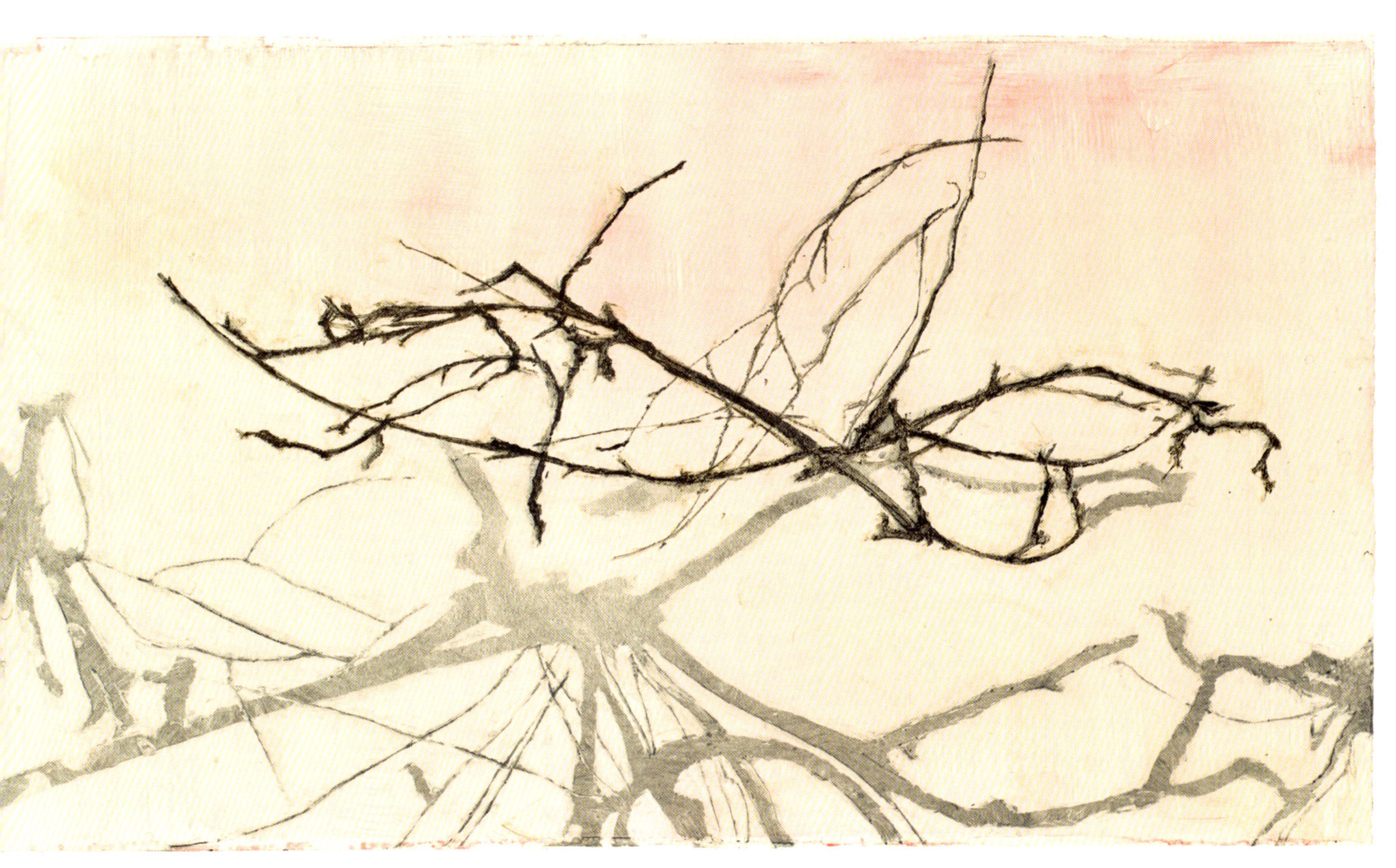

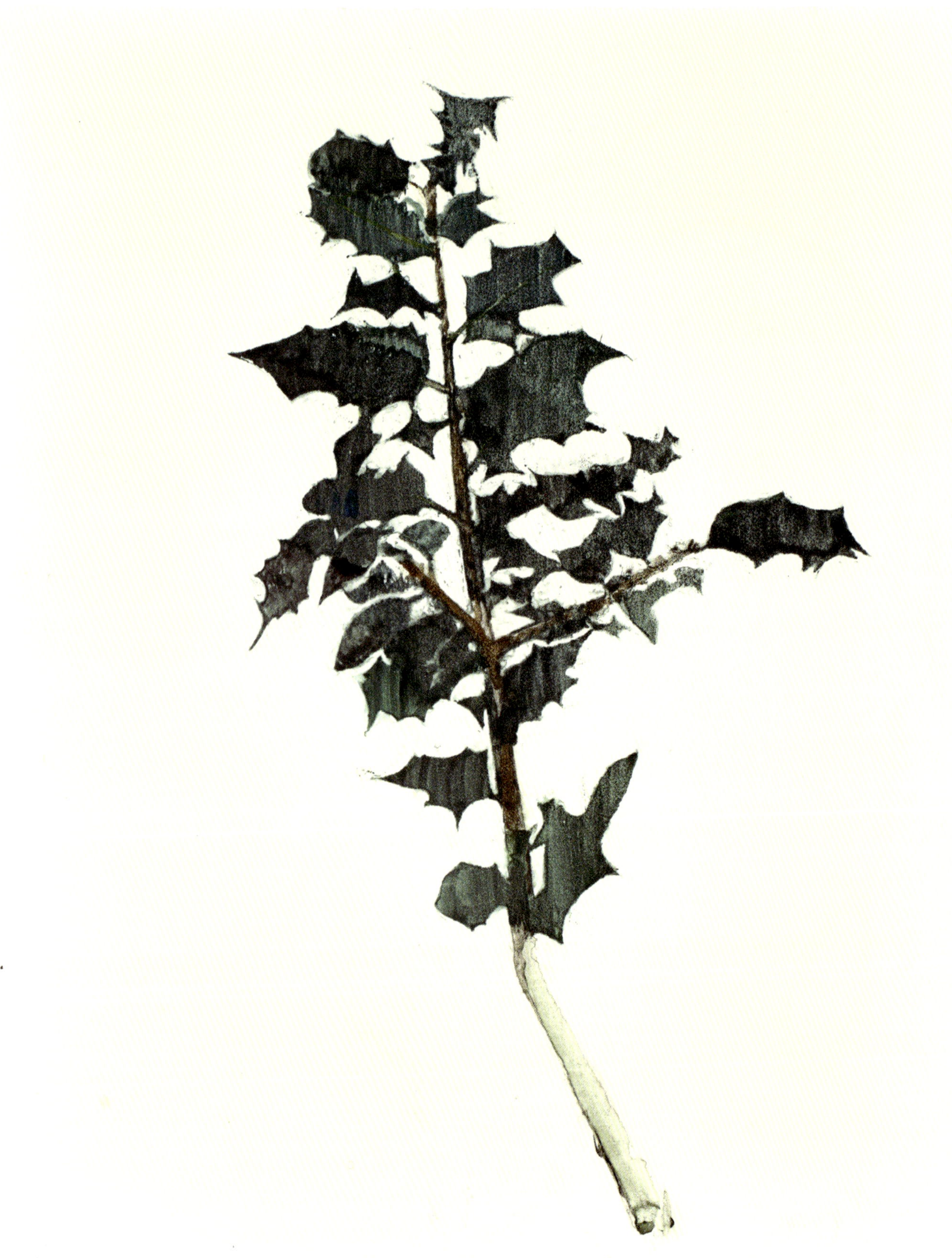

    CV98, 2021   watercolour monotype, 40.4 × 33.1 cm

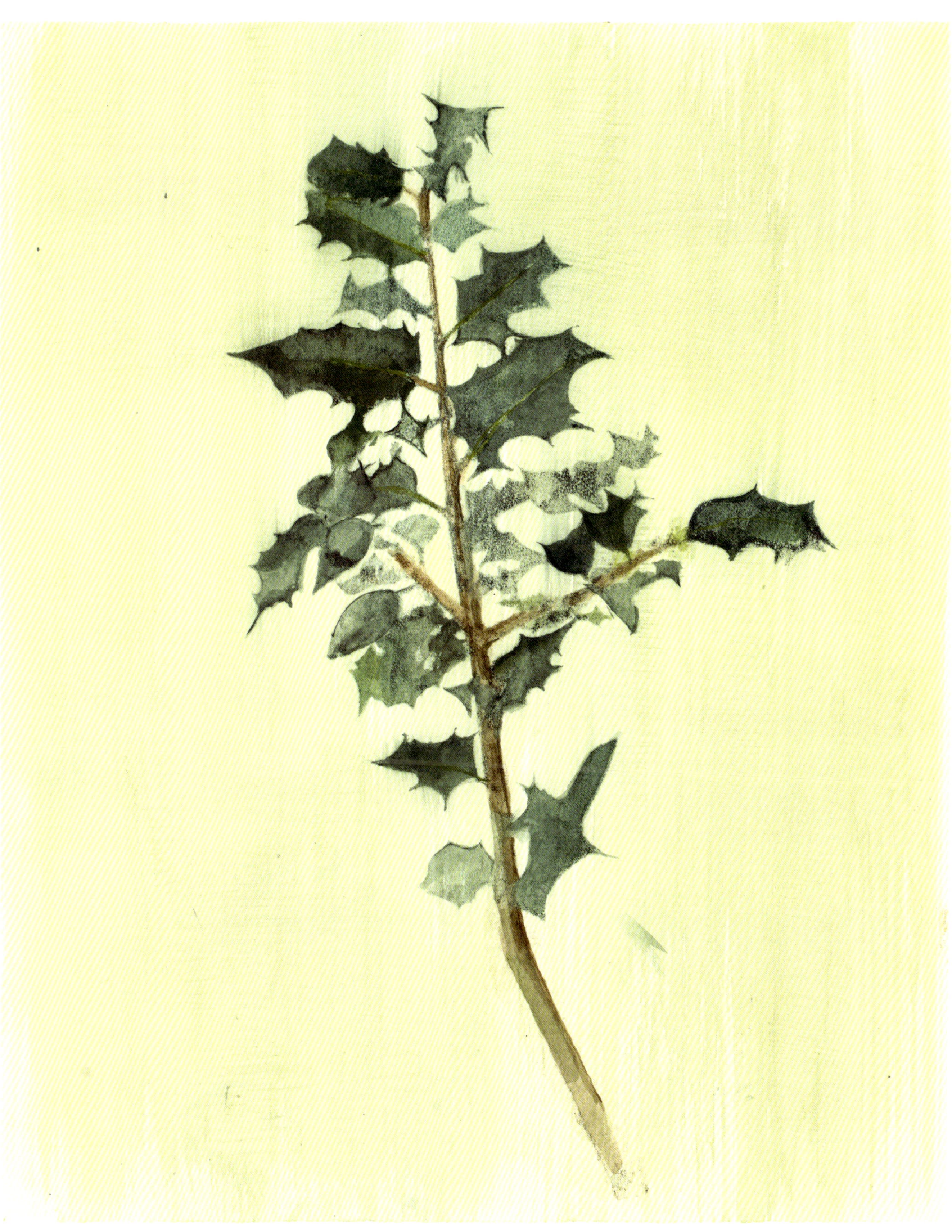

   CV100, 2021   watercolour monotype, 28.6 × 50.3 cm

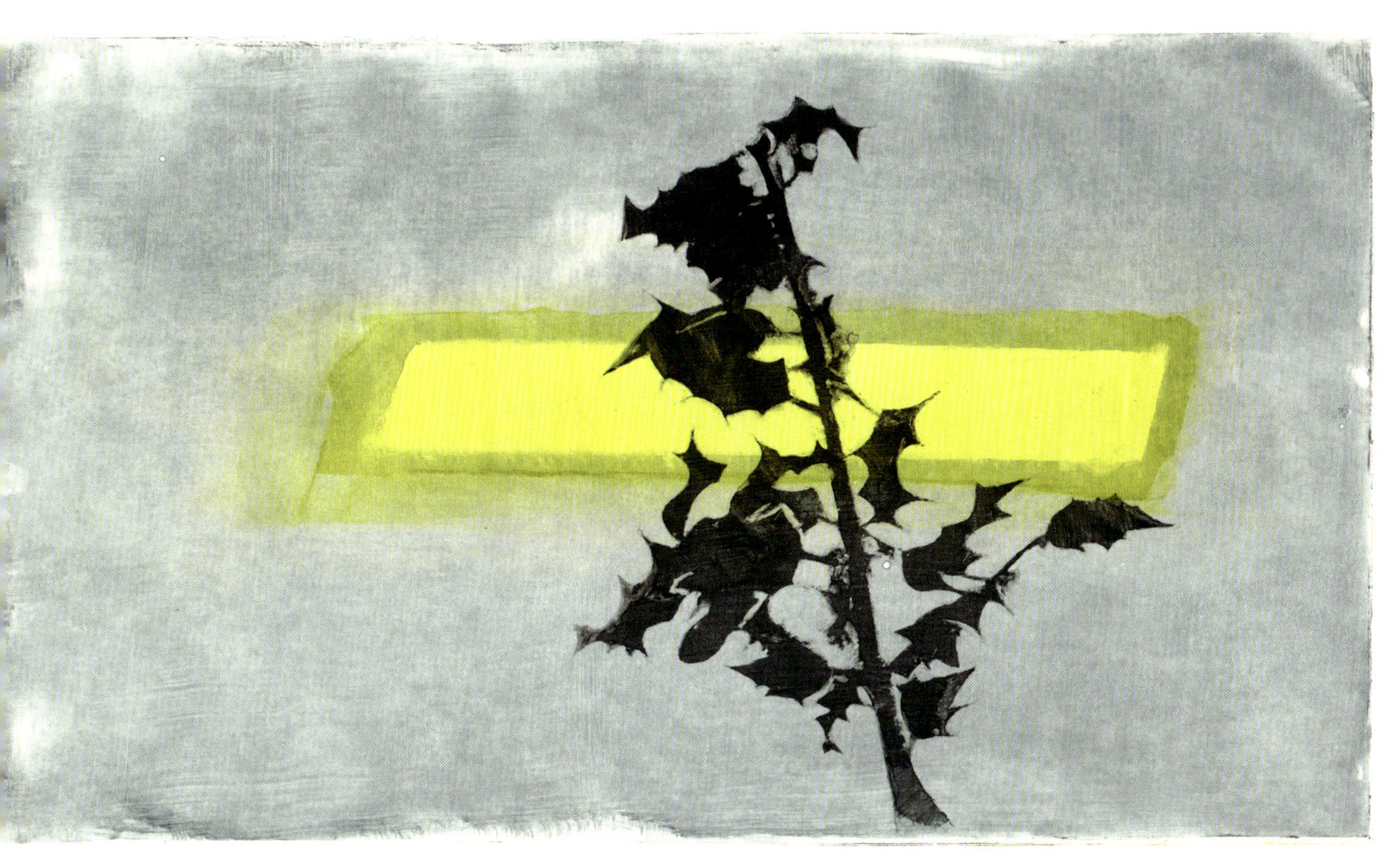

 CV101, 2021   watercolour monotype, 28.6 × 20.6 cm

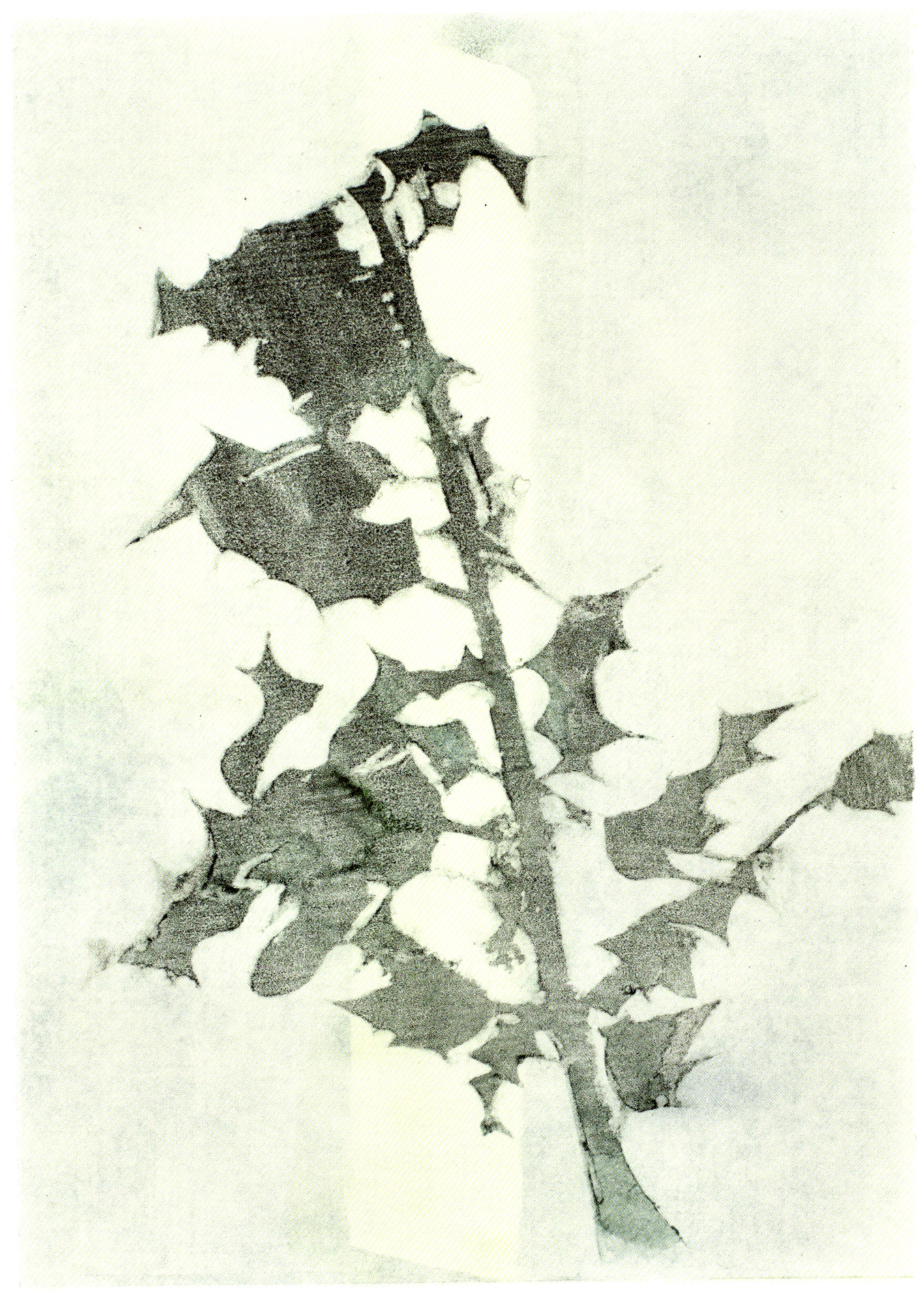

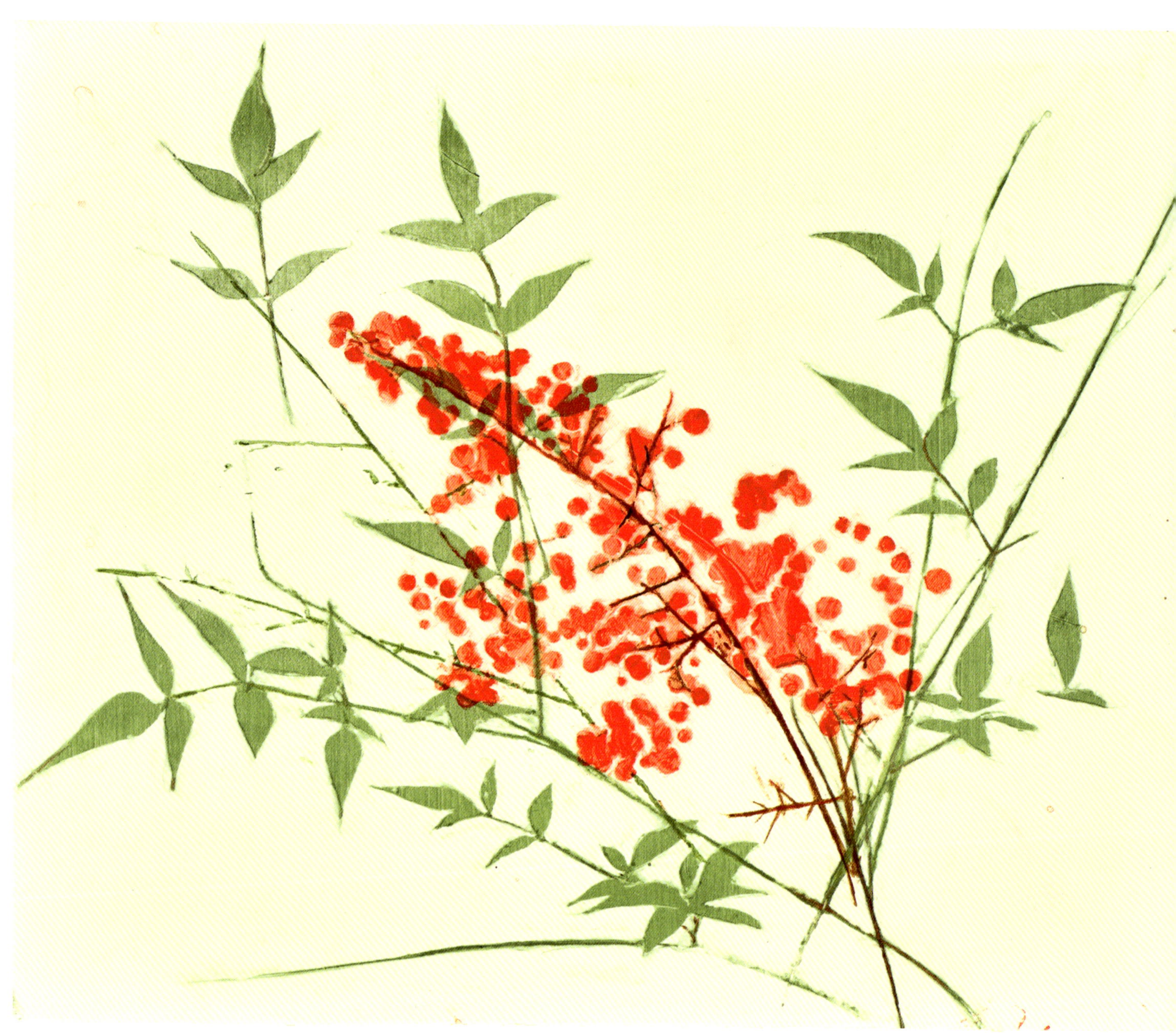

130   *CV102*, 2021   watercolour monotype, 33.2 × 40.3 cm

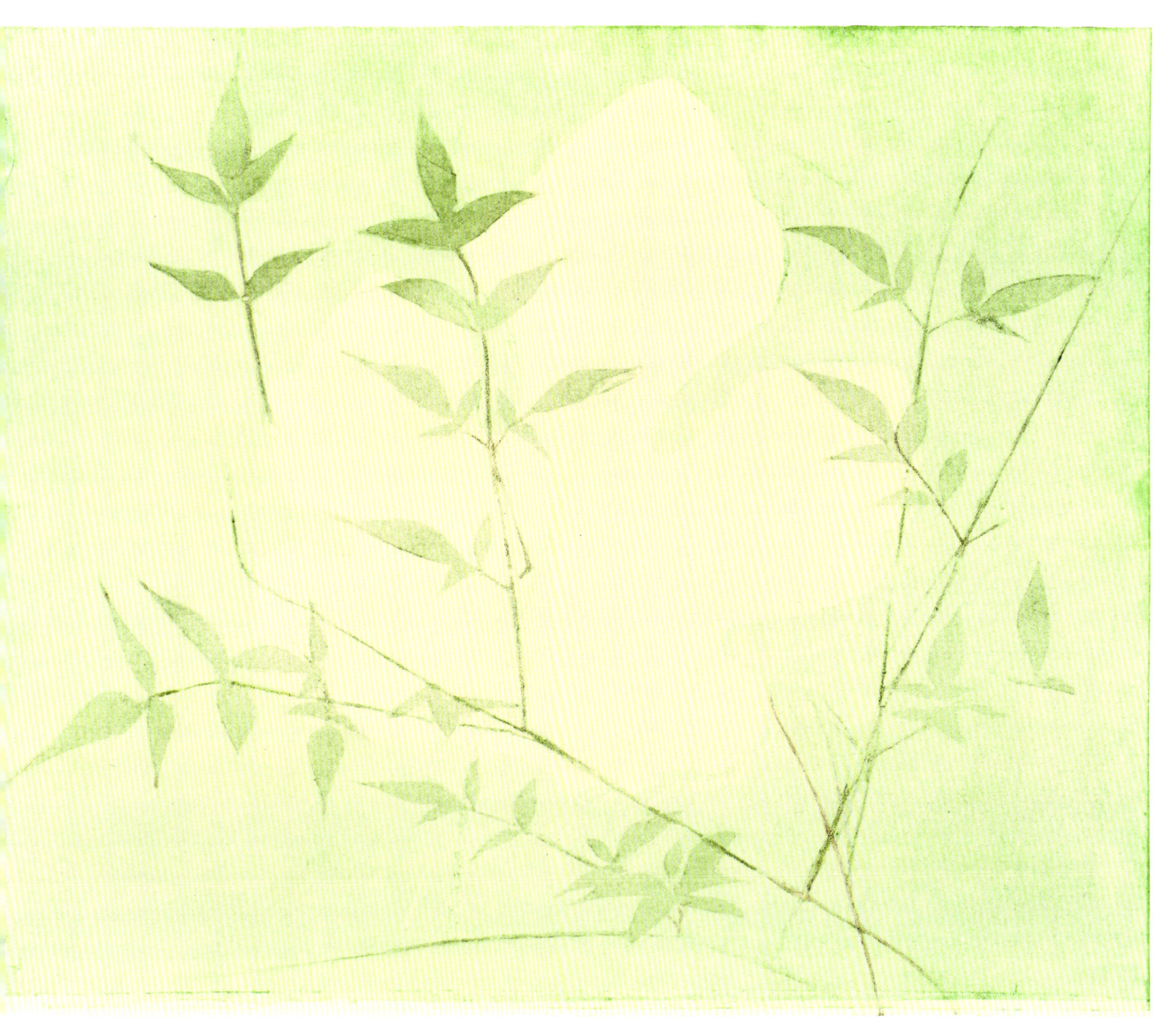

About the artist

Charlotte Verity is an observational painter who draws
on the natural world for her motifs. The works arise
from the immediate surroundings of her London
garden and are painted on the spot, either outside
or in the studio. Despite the fleeting nature of what
she depicts, the paintings develop slowly and have a
suggestion of deep space and the wider world.

Verity won the Slade Prize and Boise Travelling
Scholarship in 1977, and has since exhibited nationally
and internationally. Group exhibitions include the
Whitechapel Open, the Hayward Annual, the John
Moores, the Royal Academy Summer Exhibition, the
Drawing Room, London, in the UK, and LA Louver
and Yale Center for British Art in the USA. Her solo
shows have been with Anne Berthoud Gallery, Browse
and Darby, The North House Gallery, the Garden
Museum, London, where she was Artist in Residence
during 2010, Purdy Hicks, The New Art Centre and
Karsten Schubert London. Her work is in many public
collections including University College London,
MoCA San Diego, The Arts Council of Great Britain,
the Garden Museum, Tate Education, Deutsche Bank
and Sir John Soane's Museum.

She has been a visiting tutor at the Royal Drawing
School since 2001.

A monograph was published by Ridinghouse in 2016.

CV1 Holly and winter jasmine
CV2 Holly and winter jasmine
CV3 Winter flowering cherry
CV4 Snowdrops
CV5 Holly and winter jasmine
CV6 Holly
CV7 Snowdrops
CV8 Holly
CV9 Winter flowering cherry
CV10W Winter flowering cherry
CV11 Winter flowering cherry
CV13 Snowdrops
CV14 Winter flowering cherry
CV15 Winter flowering cherry and silver birch
CV16 Snowdrops
CV17 Snowdrops
CV19W Twig and snowdrops
CV20W Holly
CV21 Holly
CV22W Violets
CV24 Holly
CV25 Nandina and silver birch
CV26 Nandina, holly and violets
CV27 Daffodils and violets
CV28 Leucojum, violets and silver birch
CV29W Leucojum, violets and silver birch
CV30 Leucojum and grape hyacinths
CV31 Leucojum, violets and silver birch
CV32 Nandina and grape hyacinths
CV33 Pear blossom
CV35 Silver birch
CV36 Pear blossom and silver birch
CV37 Grape hyacinths and silver birch
CV38 Pear blossom and silver birch
CV39 Pear blossom
CV40 Pear blossom
CV41W Pear blossom
CV42W Pear blossom
CV43 Pear blossom
CV44 Tulip
CV45 Crab apple blossom
CV46 Crab apple blossom
CV48 Rosebuds
CV49 Tulip and silver birch

CV50 Apple blossom
CV51 Apple blossom
CV52 Apple blossom
CV53 Roses
CV55 Rosebud
CV56 Roses and love-in-a-mist
CV57 Roses
CV58 Roses
CV59 Love-in-a-mist
CV60 Love-in-a-mist
CV61 Roses and acer
CV62 Roses and acer
CV63 Nandina and plumbago
CV64 Rose stem
CV65 Plumbago and nasturtiums
CV66 Nasturtiums
CV67 Sunflowers, Japanese anemones and daisies
CV70 Japanese anemones and daisies
CV72 Fuchsia
CV73 Japanese anemones
CV75 Fuchsia and rose leaves
CV77 Fuchsia and nasturtiums
CV78 Fuchsia and rose leaves
CV79 Fuchsia
CV80 Acer
CV81 Acer
CV83 Acer
CV84 Fig leaves
CV86 Fig leaf
CV87 Fig leaf
CV88 Ivy berries and silver birch
CV90 Silver birch
CV91 Silver birch and ivy
CV92 Snowdrop
CV93 Snowdrop
CV94W Snowdrops
CV95 Snowdrops
CV96 Silver birch and pear branches
CV98 Holly
CV99W Holly
CV100 Holly
CV101 Holly
CV102 Nandina
CV103 Nandina and fig leaf

Acknowledgements

Joseph Goody printed every print and introduced me
to the technique. Nicola Togneri, with the help of Kami
Naglik, skilfully steered the project through with
dedication and enthusiasm. Tom Rowland of Karsten
Schubert London agreed to show the work for the
first time. Together with CeCe Manganaro and Kostas
Synodis they make an excellent team. Mark Thomson
designed this book with elegance and a sure touch.
It was a pleasure to work with the writer Rachel Giles
whose open and generous approach has resulted in a
text of remarkable clarity. Sophie Kullmann, publisher
of Ridinghouse, put us all together and worked
tirelessly to make this book happen. I am sincerely
grateful to them all.

As ever, my profound thanks go to Christopher Le Brun.

Published in 2021 by Ridinghouse
46 Lexington Street
London W1F 0LP
United Kingdom
ridinghouse.co.uk

Published to coincide with the exhibition
*Charlotte Verity: Echoing Green Part II:
The Printed Year*, at Karsten Schubert London,
Room 2, 18 August–10 September 2021

Distributed in the UK and Europe by
Cornerhouse Publications
c/o Home
2 Tony Wilson Place
Manchester M15 4FN
United Kingdom
cornerhousepublications.org

Distributed in rest of world by
ARTBOOK | D.A.P.
75 Broad Street, Suite 630
New York, New York 10004
artbook.com

British Library Cataloguing-in-
   Publication Data
A full catalogue record of this book is
   available from the British Library.

ISBN 978 1 909932 67 8

Ridinghouse Publisher: Sophie Kullmann
Edited by Sophie Kullmann and Aimee Selby
Proofread by Linda Schofield

Designed by Mark Thomson
Set in Lexicon (Bram de Does)

Printed in Belgium by die Keure

Cover: *CV93*, 2020
watercolour monotype, 27.9 × 20.7 cm

Ridinghouse